Smoking Assessment &
Nicotine-Free Cessation

Frederick M. Greenleaf

Abstract

This study assessed the effectiveness of a Function-Based cessation assessment and protocol in the absence of nicotine replacement against a progressive and resetting VoucherBased protocol. The assessment utilized a 5-point Likert for the 144 questions across four functions, six sub-categories, and six questions. If participants were unsuccessful in titrating down in tandem with their individualized behavior plan on a regular schedule (e.g., 25%, 50%, 75%, or 100%), they would advance to a Voucher-Based treatment. This study lasted between 3 and 12 weeks for four participants. Function-Based treatment was shown to be effective at reducing relative to baseline in all three participants that completed the study, with one participant remaining abstinent at follow-up. Of the two participants that were unsuccessful in Function-Based treatment, their frequency of continued to drop while in Voucher-Based treatment, and frequency of for those participants remained partially suppressed at onemonth follow up.

Table of content

Chapter 1: Introduction

The behavior of may have unintended long-term consequences including a loss of socially mediated reinforcement, reduction in health, financial cost, and other negative effects upon society such as those of second-hand smoke. Common treatments for cessation are nicotine patches or nicotine replacement gum, which are available in most convenience stores. Other interventions include quitting "cold turkey," chewing on toothpicks/matchsticks, slowly reducing the number of cigarettes consumed per day, and pharmacological treatments. Some of these interventions may be effective in assisting some individuals quit . In cases in which treatment is ineffective, the above interventions may be addressing a variable that is not functionally related to the behavior of .

In the field of applied behavior analysis, the typical method of behavior change is manipulation of environmental variables (e.g., maintaining consequence) to directly address a behavior's function. In the event served a function of escape from work (e.g., a break), and the individual used nicotine replacement, this intervention would not be considered function-based. The patches may however address a function of nicotine access by creating an abolishing operation (AO) defined by Cooper et al. (2020) as "a MO that decreases the current effectiveness of a reinforcer" (p. 263). If the individual's behavior as referenced above was solely maintained by access to nicotine, the use of patches may be an effective intervention, and presumably the behavior would occur less often or be fully suppressed if it was implemented. Interventions can however affect behavior in multiple ways; for example, nicotine patches may also function as a discriminative stimulus followed in the past by punishment in the sense that cigarette while wearing patches may have made the individual sick or affected heart rate. In that case, nicotine patches may be effective regardless of the function of

the behavior. This example only considers one potential function of behavior, and as a result, if the behavior is multiply maintained, a treatment package with several interventions used concurrently may be essential.

From a historical perspective, Rigotti (2012) referenced two types of cessation methodologies. These methodologies include non-pharmacologic and pharmacologic treatment. Some examples of non-pharmacologic interventions for cessation include in-person counseling (either individual or group), telephone quit lines, physician-assisted interventions such as brief advice to quit, or brief counseling. Pharmacologic interventions can include Bupropion, Varenicline, Nortriptyline, Clonidine, or nicotine replacement (patches, gum, lozenges, inhalers, and nasal spray). In general, none of these interventions inherently include a systematic measurement of behavior in order to assess effectiveness. Data are only anecdotal (self-reported) and are not systematically analyzed. Rigotti (2012) explained that cessation efforts are twice as effective when using pharmacological treatment, although risks and side effects may exist with pharmacological treatment modalities. Additionally, the author discussed the tobacco industry and e-cigarettes and other tobacco products. An individual may attempt to quit by engaging in an alternative topography (e.g., different types of tobacco) and still be a customer to the tobacco industry. Lastly, Rigotti mentioned that only a third of individuals utilize any treatment assistance. In other words, two thirds of individuals employ a quitting "cold turkey" approach and may not result in long term cessation. In general, interventions mentioned in the literature appear to be chosen arbitrarily without consideration of function. A singular treatment in isolation may or may not help an individual quit , as it may or may not directly address the behavior's function. Currently, there is a dearth of behavior-analytic literature on functional assessments for . Assessments of behavior from a clinical perspective exist, but don't directly address the function of or inform an evidence-based best-practice treatment. The study attempted to address this gap in research and practice.

Assessment of

Frederiksen et al. (1979) identified methods by which to measure the behavior of during assessment. Some of these measures became dependent variables for this study. Data collected include frequency of , topography of , and levels of tar, smoke, and nicotine in the participant's body. Useful dimensions of measurement may vary across individuals (e.g., duration of inhale, amount of nicotine consumed, etc.). The authors suggested tracking three dimensions of : frequency, substance, and topography.

Self-report measures regarding may provide ample information regarding frequency, substance, and topography, although self-report measures may suffer from some limitations such as accuracy and reliability of the reports. For frequency tracking, the number of cigarettes smoked per day may be self-recorded, and also the times each of these instances occur. Powell and Azrin (1968) automated frequency measures by developing a cigarette case that counts the number of times the case itself is opened, although these automations (reducing other limitations) may create more in the instance the cigarette case could break, or if multiple cigarettes were removed at once. Measurement of substances could include reporting of cigarette brand. Topographical measurement could include frequency of puffs during a given instance of , puff duration, inter-response time between puffs cigarette duration, puff volume, puff intensity, puff distribution, etc.

Frederiksen et al. (1979) also discussed physiological measures such as carbon monoxide (CO) monitoring (measured by exhale) and Cotinine analysis (measured by saliva sample), which result in more objective data than self-report. Bancroft (1997) suggested self-report data may include bias, especially for "sensitive or illegal behavior" (p. 41), although selfadministered testing or retesting may mitigate some of these effects. With this in mind, selfreport measures for the behavior of should be corroborated through self-administered testing in this study.

Currently-available cessation assessments in the medical field, such as the Fagerstrom Test for Nicotine Dependence (Heatherton et al., 1991), the Questionnaire of
Urges (QSU; Tiffany & Drobes, 1991), and the Minnesota Nicotine Withdrawal Questionnaire (MNWQ; Hughes & Hatsukami, 1986) may not directly address all antecedents to behavior that are relevant to individuals with diverse learning histories. In addition, these indirect assessments do not necessarily address the direct consequences (which may be maintaining variables) of the behavior either, which is why this study offered a novel contribution. The brief version of the Fagerstrom Test for Nicotine Dependence assesses frequency of , when the occurs, the effect of location, and whether internal events (e.g., sickness) may affect . The QSU assesses drives to smoke (i.e., how much does the individual want to smoke in the moment and in the future). Lastly, the MNWQ assesses internal states related to such as being angry, anxious, depressed, and restless.

With these assessments in mind, it is important to develop assessment of environmental stimuli not only that may maintain behavior, but that may lead to behavior being occasioned and/or evoked. Antecedents that both evoke (i.e., increase the frequency of a behavior that has previously been reinforced by a stimulus that is increased in reinforcing value) and occasion (i.e., increase responding as a result of being previously correlated with reinforcement) should be considered during assessment (Cooper et al., 2020). Function-based treatment directly manipulates maintaining, evoking, and occasioning variables, whereas currently common treatments are more arbitrarily selected and may not be universally applicable to all individuals' behavior. The use of nicotine patches assumes that the behavior of is maintained by access to nicotine, whereas there may be several other maintaining variables, and nicotine access may not even be a maintaining variable. Patch ineffectiveness for a given individual may lend itself to this notion. In all, function-based treatments are preferable as they are customized to the unique environments of each individual and may be more immediately and reliably effective. Additionally, function-based treatments do not rely on punishment to reduce frequency of a particular behavior, and these treatments may be paired with reinforcement procedures for an alternative response.

There is dearth of literature on function-based interventions for cessation. Axelrod (1991) described the use of an indirect functional assessment as related to the modification and/or treatment of undesirable, potentially dangerous behavior. The author suggested that non-behavior analysts do use tools that seem to address some potential functional relations for the behavior of . *The Wellness Encyclopedia* (1991) (Appendix A) includes various techniques for medical professionals to promote healthy lifestyles and prevent illness; some of these pertain to assessment and treatment of , as shown in Appendix A. The assessment provided in the appendix is sometimes given by medical professionals prior to selecting a treatment to promote cessation. Interventions typically are nonetheless not based on behavior function. Axelrod (1991) suggested that behavior analysts take steps to assist medical professionals in selecting evidence-based treatment for cessation. Axelrod

(1991) was the first to reference this topic in behavior-analytic literature and discussed variables potentially functionally related to ; this study attempted to inform treatment based on an in-depth functional assessment including these variables and others.

Behavior-analytic practitioners use tools called functional behavior assessments (FBAs) of which there are three types, all referenced in by Cooper et al. (2020). These assessment types are indirect, direct, and experimental. Indirect assessments involve interviewing a client, participant, or surrogate, or providing questionnaires about behavior and environmental context to identify a behavior's potential function. An example of this could be a questionnaire asking how many cigarettes that individual smokes per day and the times they engage in that behavior, as well as the interviewee's interpretation of what environmental events accompany behavior. Direct assessments involve observation and recording of the antecedents and consequences of a target behavior in an attempt to identify the behavior's potential function; an example here is observing the individual within their natural environment and recording the antecedents and consequences of the behavior. Lastly, experimental assessments are called functional analyses (FAs).

During these assessments, variables that may be evoking,

occasioning, or maintaining a behavior are directly manipulated to

isolate effects upon behavior.

Experimental functional analyses are a tool used to repeatedly
demonstrate a cause and effect

(i.e., functional) relationship to determine a behavior's maintaining

consequences and occasioning or evoking antecedents (Iwata &

Dozier, 2008). This experimental demonstration is the gold standard

for identifying behavior function but may not be practical for given

this behavior may occur in all environments instead of in isolation

(e.g., only at home or only at work).

For , isolating maintaining variables may be problematic as

these behaviors may occur throughout the day (as levels of

deprivation increase and decrease). Additionally, the behavior may

occur across many settings in the natural environment, which could

include incredibly large amounts of evoking or occasioning stimuli.

At the same time, Axelrod (1991) stated "given the interest that

physicians demonstrate in conducting functional analyses of

behavior, behavior analysts can make significant contributions to the approach by introducing rigorous measurement procedures and research designs" (p. 718). This study was focused on the development of an indirect functional assessment specifically geared toward the behavior of . The indirect assessment developed for the purpose of this study included questionnaires implemented during one-on-one interviews with clients. These questionnaires included questions correlated with specific potential functions of behavior. When responses were coded, this assessment recommended empirically-supported function-based treatment. In effect, components of existing empirically validated assessments and treatments were optimized by using the science of behavior to identify and systematically manipulate the maintaining variables for , and hopefully increase treatment efficacy as compared to standard treatment.

A History of Non-Function-Based Treatment of

Much of the current behavior-analytic literature on from the *Journal of Applied Behavior Analysis* (1968-2013) does not directly address function-based treatment, but instead focuses on voucher-based reinforcement and various methods of punishment given that there is not currently a robust function based assessment for .

Punishment procedures are not function-based, nor are voucher

systems, which rely on generalized conditioned reinforcement (GCR).

Punishment-based procedures (e.g., shock, rapid , cognitive control,

etc.) may be implemented without reinforcement components at all.

Voucher-based reinforcement may also inherently include aversive

control. In cases of resetting contingencies and contingent loss of

reinforcers, when participants cease , they effectively are avoiding the

loss of potential sources of reinforcement, a form of negative

reinforcement.

Punishment procedures are environmental changes which are

highly effective in decreasing future rates of behavior that are

currently occurring when an aversive stimulus is presented either at

the same time as the target behavior or immediately following

(Lerman & Vorndran, 2002). At the same time, these interventions

may not just decrease future rates of the target behavior; they may

actually punish other responses in the same response class hierarchy.

Balsam and Bondy (1983) explained this concept by noting that "the

consequence of a response affects all operant classes to which the response belongs. In the case of punishment, a particular target response might be suppressed, but so might other responses that belong to the same operant class" (p. 286). In addition, there are many other unintended effects of punishment procedures. Just because one member of a response class is punished does not mean all members would reduce in frequency; other members may actually increase in frequency. If one member of a response class is punished or blocked, other topographies may increase in rate due to the variables affecting a response class hierarchy (e.g., aggression, screaming, and self-injury), as demonstrated by Lalli et al. (1995). Other topographies may increase in rate due to the variables affecting a response class hierarchy. In a different case, if the response is punished in environment one but there is no contingent punishment in environment two, the response may increase in rate in environment two due to the stimulus control. This phenomenon is called behavioral contrast, as described by Brethower and Reynolds (1962). Additionally, punishment procedures used in isolation do not train more preferable alternative responses, which means another undesirable behavior that serves the same function may appear and subsequently become reinforced.

The ethical guidelines for behavior analysts stipulate that minimally obtrusive procedures to suppress responding (e.g., by training functional alternatives) should be attempted prior to using punishment procedures, as these procedures are more obtrusive and restrictive than other reinforcement-based procedures (Bailey & Burch, 2011). Code 4.08 of the Behavior Analyst's Code of Ethics also stipulates "Behavior analysts recommend reinforcement rather than punishment whenever possible" (Behavior Analyst Certification Board, 2016, p. 13). The efficacy of punishment may be increased when reinforcement is concurrently available as demonstrated by Thompson et al. (1999), where the effects of restraint suppressed self-injurious behavior further when access to reinforcement (leisure materials) was contingent upon alternative responding. Punishment procedures are easily administered and even without a continuous schedule (which is most effective) can still suppress responding, which is one reason why they are used despite maximal intrusiveness.

Presentation of aversive stimuli may also have other unintended negative side effects. These effects may include punishment-induced emotional and aggressive responding, the mediator of punishment beginning to function as an aversive stimulus themselves, alternative responses in the same response class increasing (e.g., if you punish cigarettes, a person may use a pipe or chewing tobacco), emergence of new escape and/or avoidant responses, suppression of desirable behavior in close temporal proximity, or conditioning undesirable respondent behavior (e.g., anxiety responses; Lerman & Vorndran, 2002). Function-based treatments, however, address the root causes of behavior without as many negative side effects. By using function-based treatments, alternative stimuli (e.g., matched or competing stimuli) may be presented in the absence of the target behavior of to produce long term behavioral changes without utilizing aversive stimuli. With all of this in mind, function-based reinforcement or antecedent manipulation procedures are ideal.

Function-based reinforcement is preferable to Generalized Conditioned Reinforcement (GCR) as GCRs only maintain their value as long as they are intermittently paired with other forms of conditioned or unconditioned reinforcement and can continue to be exchanged for other primary and secondary reinforcers. In addition, if GCRs are paired with few other reinforcers, they are effective only if there is some form of deprivation for the reinforcers paired with them (e.g., the tokens utilized in the study by Moher et al., 2008). These GCRs must also be of a greater value than the maintaining consequence to promote alternative responding, assuming there is also no punitive contingency that coexists. Emission of alternative responses is a function of effort, learning history, schedules of reinforcement, and likelihood of punishment (Lalli et al., 1995). Function-based reinforcement addresses precisely what is maintaining the behavior, and a manipulation of a maintaining variable would have much greater long-term efficacy.

Silverman et al. (2008) reviewed evidence-based treatments for cessation. First and foremost, Silverman et al. (2008) highlighted that the majority of literature in the *Journal of Applied Behavior Analysis* has employed non-function-based interventions to promote cessation. The intent of this study was to do just that: identify potential functions of behavior, develop an assessment to accurately identify the functions affecting individuals' behavior, and use the results of the assessment to tailor function-based approaches. In the end, Silverman et al. (2008) noted that only a small amount of research on the topic of cessation has been published in the *Journal of Applied Behavior Analysis*. The authors referenced contingency management in the form of arranging GCR contingencies as the mostresearched methodology for cessation. These procedures have been shown to be generally effective at promoting cessation. However, GCR loss creates a potential aversive contingency. In effect, if participants smoke they lose the opportunity of the GCR's presentation, a form of negative punishment. Additionally, if an individual was to engage in behavior maintained by avoidance of the loss of a GCR, the behavior would also be maintained by another form of an aversive contingency (negative reinforcement).

Another limitation to contingency management is that to present GCRs, you often must have a mediator, which may not be necessary when utilizing some function-based treatments unless a function of access to attention exists. Additionally, with GCRs, researchers have created contingencies that compete with the behavior of , without directly training functional alternatives. Another concern is that when a schedule of GCRs is no longer in place, the efficacy of treatment may not maintain if the reinforcement system is not properly faded. When using function-based treatment that includes differential reinforcement of an alternative behavior that is reinforced in the natural environment, long-term cessation may be more likely to maintain (Piazza et al., 1996).

Another issue that has made using contingency management less feasible in applied environments is the cost of the program, especially when the literature suggests increased magnitude of a reinforcer increases the reinforcer efficacy. Other researchers such as Romanowich and Lamb (2010) and Alessi et al. (2008) have attempted to address this cost with several solutions (e.g., varying the magnitude of the reinforcer, or earning draws from a fishbowl to earn prizes), none of which have been empirically demonstrated to save money and may actually reduce effectiveness.

With that being said, of the contingency management programs discussed, voucher-based reinforcement was found to be the most effective treatment procedure (Silverman et al., 2008). In this study, the effects of function-based interventions were compared to those of voucher-based reinforcement. In addition, costs aside, web-based contingency management has been shown to be an effective tool to promote abstinence by allowing individuals to submit CO results online at convenient times. The consideration here is that results of CO monitoring can only test for abstinence within the past several hours, which means multiple samples would be required daily in order to determine adherence. The main dependent variable in this study was CO levels, tracked the same way as much of the existing literature with monitoring multiple times each day, in addition to intermittent cotinine measurement, paired with tracking the number of cigarettes daily. Some researchers have also included social support applications to use in conjunction with contingency management. Social support was certainly needed to be a component for functionbased interventions that require others' presence, such as in the case of Foxx and Brown (1979), included in this study's literature review.

Other topics of cessation research in *The Journal of Applied Behavior Analysis* have included locking cigarette cases (e.g., Azrin

& Powell, 1968). As a punishment procedure, function is not addressed; contingent upon opening a cigarette case, the case will lock. Another is nicotine fading (e.g., Foxx & Brown, 1979) which assumes nicotine is the maintaining variable without necessarily relying on initial functional assessment; participants in the cited study were instructed to smoke cigarettes with progressively less nicotine. In the case of Acceptance and commitment therapy (ACT; e.g., Twohig et al., 2007) function is again not directly addressed based on functional assessment. In the cited study, participants were instructed to engage in a talk therapy-based approach to behavior change. ACT could assist in guiding individuals to take committed action to remove paraphernalia in their environment in addition to accepting the potential discomfort with breaking behavioral chains of (e.g., by engaging in alternative responses), where in the past they would have engaged in behavior. These antecedent-based interventions may be function-based depending on the variables affecting a given individual's behavior, but these variables would need to be identified via assessment.

The addition of any of the above interventions may be useful supplements to a functionbased treatment package. In particular, the addition of a fading plan, a component commonly used in voucher-based systems, can help to ensure that treatment effects maintain over time. A useful dependent measure when using nicotine fading may be percent of each cigarette smoked and type (brand) of cigarette butts turned in (Foxx & Brown, 1979). Nicotine fading likely addresses the single variable of nicotine itself as a maintaining function for the behavior of . Foxx and Brown (1979) found that social support plus nicotine fading was the best intervention of those that they assessed; 40% of participants were abstinent at an 18-month follow up. These data may suggest the two intervention components in conjunction addressed two potential functions: nicotine access and attention. This study used its assessment to determine many, if not all potential sources of reinforcement, and target many, if not all possible functions in conjunction. The objective of using several components within a treatment package is to promote long-term maintenance and generalization across many different types of stimuli and environments. For example, if nicotine patches function as an abolishing operation decreasing the likelihood of the behavior of , but do not completely suppress this behavior in the presence of other individuals (an evoking or occasioning stimulus), the addition of teaching a functionally equivalent competing or incompatible response may prevent from occurring.

For behavior analysis to have a substantive impact on the treatment of , the behavior must be assessed in terms of its environmental context and all of the effects the activity has on an individual's public and private environments. An environment includes, but is not limited to socially mediated consequences in addition to the biological effects. Analyzing these consequences allow clinicians to identify potential functions and develop customized treatment for each individual. At this time, no such assessment exists.

Chapter 2: Review of the Literature

Punishment Procedures

Powell and Azrin (1968) assessed the effect of shock as a punisher contingent upon opening a specially designed cigarette case. Participants wore a device that would deliver shock on a continuous schedule of punishment and also to automatically count the number of times the cigarette case was opened. Secondly, individuals in the participant's environment tracked the participant's behavior of . The dependent variable in this study was the number of cigarettes smoked. While this was also measured by case opening, the participant could have received several cigarettes or not reset the electrical rod when closing the case. Additionally, these participants may have procured cigarettes from elsewhere. Lastly, the experimenters found in prior research that working with individuals rather than groups would be more effective.

Through parametric testing, several shock magnitudes were used for each participant

(Powell & Azrin, 1968). behavior was measured before, during, and after treatment. The apparatus included a cigarette case, electrode case, and the electrical stimulator. The case had a non-resettable counter, and the participants were given a sheet of paper attached to the case to record the time of the behavior when it occurred. There were five steps in this experiment: self-monitoring, reading literature on effects of , wearing the apparatus with no shock, shock punishment with progressive increases in magnitude, and withdrawal of shock. For the progressive shock magnitude increase, shock magnitude was increased until behavior suppression was seen.

The experimenters found that cigarette may be suppressed using shock, with increased shock magnitude having a greater effect on suppression (Powell & Azrin, 1968). The findings were that when shock was removed, the participants' rate returned to prepunishment levels, and that only decreased when the shock magnitude reached a level that would actually fully suppress behavior. What this tells researchers is that the shock was not truly a punisher at low magnitudes. The authors made several considerations suggesting that shock may not have been the stimulus that actually suppressed the behavior. Providing information on the dangers of may have suppressed behavior or made the behavior more sensitive to subsequent intervention. In addition, the novel stimulus of shock in and of itself could produce suppression; the contingent stimulation may not have needed to be as shock.

Lastly, confounding variables in the participants' lives may have influenced suppression, which is also true for any applied intervention.

Azrin and Powell (1968) assessed the effects of using a self-locking cigarette case, such that when a participant opened the cigarette case and removed any number of cigarettes, the case would close and lock for a set period of time. The procedure is in itself a negative punishment procedure (i.e., loss of the reinforcer for a set period of time) contingent upon opening the case, and the behavior of opening the case would be placed on extinction during a fixed interval schedule. The experiment used a changing criterion design which increased the time for which the case was locked. The authors discussed prior research in which a case presented a shock contingent upon opening the case. As to be expected, the case came to function as an aversive stimulus, and the participants readily discontinued the use of the apparatus, which prompted the authors to address the suppressive effects related to extinction instead. The experimental questions related to whether participants would use the case and whether participants would continue with the procedure, and the dependent measure was the number of cigarettes smoked.

> The total duration of the study ranged between 7-12 weeks depending on the participant

(3 in experimental condition, and 2 in control; Azrin & Powell, 1968). To begin, the authors took baseline data on the inter-response time (IRT) of case-opening to set the initial criterion for the case to be locked. The first step in the experiment lasted anywhere from 4-10 days across all participants. The case was locked contingent upon removing a cigarette for the total duration   a cigarette, which lasted approximately 6 min. The purpose of this procedure was to get the subjects used to using the apparatus while not interrupting the number of potential cigarettes smoked. The apparatus tracked the number of times the case was opened and the participants also were given a card by which they would record the time of day and the counter readings. In addition, there were individuals in the participant's environment who would also track the participant's . Two participants were in the control condition, which involved using a

"Memosmoke" device, where the participant themselves set the lock duration as opposed to it being experimenter-controlled. Every three days, the three participants in the experimental condition were given the opportunity to increase the total duration of time the case would be locked.

The results were that the "Memosmoke" device alone was not successful in reducing the number of cigarettes smoked, but the addition of the experimental procedure was effective in reducing the number of cigarettes smoked to approximately half of baseline rates (Azrin & Powell, 1968). The researchers were able to systematically decrease the number of cigarettes smoked by slowly increasing the delay between availability of cigarettes. Based on these results, aversive control may not be necessary to promote cessation if extinction may also be effective. At the same time, extinction may produce unintended effects such as extinction induced emotional responding and extinction-induced aggressive responding as described by

Azrin et al. (1966).

Dericco et al. (1977) conducted a multiple baseline component analysis across participants receiving different treatments to assess the effects of three aversive control procedures to promote cessation. These techniques included satiation, cognitive control, and contingent electric shock. The technique of satiation involved one of two separate interventions, the first being filling a room full of smoke, and the second being rapid . Both had previously shown limited effectiveness long term. Fischer et al. (1997) described satiation as presenting a maintaining consequence on a time-based schedule, independent of the targeted response, such that the frequency of targeted behavior will be suppressed, even if the response still contacts reinforcement. Over-satiation was thought to lead to the development of automatic punishment as the behavior of typical may take on the aversive properties of over-satiation (e.g., sickness), such that if the behavior occurred outside of these sessions it may be likely to contact conditioned aversive stimulation. Cognitive procedures involved imagining one was about to smoke a cigarette and then imagining an aversive stimulus, both of which never occurred. Experiments using this method had been unsuccessful long term despite short success post-treatment. Contingent electric shock had been shown to be highly effective in producing significant reductions in . However, the authors added that in the previous literature effects of this shock could not be separated from other independent variables that were run concurrently.

The participants in this study were 24 individuals, 20 to 55 years of age; each experienced one 3-part treatment condition where baseline ranged between one to six weeks depending on treatment condition (Dericco et al., 1977). The six sets of conditions included 1) SatiationCognitive Control-Satiation, 2) Cognitive Control-Satiation-Shock, 3) Shock-Shock-Cognitive

Control, 4) Satiation-Satiation-Shock, and 5) Shock-Cognitive Control-Cognitive Control, and 6) Shock-Shock-Satiation. Conditions switched when steady state responding was found across a five-day period. Each of the six treatment sequences were replicated four times. Across all six conditions, the minimum number of sessions was a mean of 28 and the maximum number of sessions was a mean of 45. Each participant recorded their daily frequency of , antecedent conditions, time of , and concurrent behaviors. Data were given to the experimenter five times per week. In baseline, subjects tracked the data referenced above for one to six weeks relative to which treatment program they were assigned to. In satiation sessions, participants were required to smoke six cigarettes independent of their own . If participants' rate fell below one cigarette within a 5-min period, they were instructed to continue . There were nine instances in which participants vomited.   In the cognitive control condition, participants listened to a tape with multiple vignettes (Dericco et al., 1977). The first vignette described laying on a beach and stated that not for two years would put the participant there. The second described being in a hospital in excruciating pain, dying of lung cancer. These tapes were played continuously thorough sessions. After sessions, participants were told to imagine these when in the future.

In the contingent shock condition, a punisher assessment was run, and depending on the level of shock at which behavior was suppressed, the experimenters increased the magnitude slightly (Dericco et al., 1977). In this condition, participants were asked to smoke at a typical rate, and shocks were presented 25 times on a variable schedule contingent upon several targeted behaviors: igniting a cigarette, holding onto a cigarette when ignited, and inhaling the ignited cigarette.

After six months, the experimenters conducted a follow-up and data were tracked in an identical manner to baseline for two weeks (Dericco et al., 1977). The findings of this experiment were that for group one who experienced satiation, cognitive control, then satiation again, there were no long lasting effects on cessation. In groups two (shock, cognitive control, cognitive control), three (cognitive control, satiation, shock), and four (satiation, satiation, shock), there was some success with long term cessation; cessation was achieved for eight of twelve participants. Group three decreased the frequency of their but did not remain abstinent by follow-up. For groups five (shock, shock, and cognitive control), and six (shock, shock, cognitive control), cessation maintained for all members in the group at six-month follow up.

The results of this study suggest a correlation between contingent electric shock and cessation (Dericco et al., 1977), which evidenced by the reduction in across group five and six. In these conditions, there were two shock series presented back to back, relative to one shock component in the other treatment packages. In addition, in shock sessions, the amount of sessions required to reach steady state responding was far less relative to other component groups. The study has shown that contingent electric shock may be an effective procedure by which to reduce the behavior of as the individuals in the two-shock condition had remained abstinent at follow-up. Additionally, even the one-shock condition reduced participants' frequency. The order of the three conditions did not influence cessation, (i.e., shock was effective whenever it occurred in the series of interventions).

An important note is that of those who remained abstinent, all had reached full suppression by the end of the shock condition (Dericco et al., 1977). Additionally, four additional shock sessions were given following full suppression. That is, shock was available, but never presented as the behavior was fully suppressed; the authors noted that this could have influenced long term maintenance of cessation. The authors also noted that there may have been a relationship between the total frequency of cigarettes smoked during baseline and the number of shock sessions needed to achieve cessation. The authors concluded with the note that these data may not be generalizable to groups whom are not willing to participate in a long-term treatment plan like referenced in this experiment.

Punishment procedures are not function-based, nor do they train alternative behaviors. The use of these procedures may punish all members in a response class but may also make other members' probability increase relative to the punished member (behavioral contrast; Brethower & Reynolds, 1962). Essentially, if a person uses multiple types of tobacco such as chew, cigarettes, or snuff, and contingent electric shock is presented following cigarette (assuming shock functions as a punisher), cigarettes may reduce in frequency while engaging in these other behaviors may increase in frequency, magnitude, etc.

Shock has been found to be highly effective for reducing many behaviors, included. At the same time, it is seen as maximally invasive and maximally restrictive (Lerman & Vorndran, 2002). In addition, many voucher-based studies have employed resetting contingencies paired with a loss of reinforcement contingent upon positive or missed CO readings, which is inherently a negative punisher. Punishment procedures and aversive stimulation by definition induces escape and avoidant responses. Punishment procedures may limit participants' adherence to a treatment protocol. Deliberately-programmed positive reinforcement increases the future likelihood of desirable behavior, whereas punishment may produce many negative side effects.

Acceptance and Commitment Therapy

Acceptance and commitment therapy (ACT) methodologies are derived from a theory of language called Relational Frame Theory. In this therapy, an individual is coached to defuse from thoughts, accept thoughts (rather than avoid), and take committed action as referenced by Hayes et al. (2012). The article by Twohig et al. (2007) examined the effects of using ACT as a treatment for marijuana . Three participants were recruited at a local university from psychology classes. The dependent variables in this study were self-report of marijuana intake and results of oral swab tests. Each participant was given a card to mark every time they smoked marijuana and to track the number of inhalations per day. Participants also completed the *Marijuana Withdrawal Checklist* (MWC), *Beck Anxiety Inventory* (BAI), *Beck Depression Inventory- II* (BDI-II), and the *Acceptance and Action Questionnaire* (AAQ). The treatment included eight 90-min weekly sessions of ACT. Some areas focused on in this therapy were an assessment of participant functioning, values work, creative hopelessness/workability, acceptance, diffusion, and committed action. The findings were that relative to baseline, participants reported large reductions in their intake of marijuana during treatment, which was also evidenced by oral swabs. The study shows that ACT may be effective in treating marijuana dependence, although data were mostly self-reported.

While Twohig and colleagues (2007) addressed a reduction in marijuana and not cigarettes, ACT may be a viable option for cessation. There is little empirical research on clinical behavioral interventions for reductions in behavior other than the study described above and a study by Dericco et al. (1977), which included a cognitive control intervention (i.e., imagining and imagining noxious/aversive stimuli to pair the two together). Roll and Howard (2008) referenced using "willpower" to quit which may be conceptualized as self-control. Self-control could be defined as doing anything to arrange one's public or private environment to reduce a behavior's frequency, magnitude, etc.

ACT is not always a function-based intervention but may be a useful intervention to create rule-governed behavior defined by Cooper and colleagues (2020) as "behavior controlled by a rule (i.e., a verbal statement of an antecedent-behavior-consequence contingency) [that] enables human behavior (e.g., fastening a seatbelt) to come under the indirect control of temporally remote or improbable but potentially significant consequences" (pg. 703). In other words, ACT can affect behavior without it contacting consequences by creating an if/then rule based in language.

Research regarding ACT and cessation is limited, but may be a socially valid treatment to address negative effects surrounding this behavior change. ACT requires committed action on the part of the client or participant, and this may or may not limit adherence to this type of treatment protocol. At any rate, mindfulness may reduce or eliminate some evoking properties related to .

Generalized Conditioned Reinforcement

Alessi et al. (2008) conducted a study which included 24 individuals who were entering a residential substance abuse clinic. These individuals were described as having some form of dependence on alcohol, cocaine, or heroin. Of these participants, all had expressed interest in also quitting in conjunction with treatment for other addiction(s). Initial assessment data were collected via an initial CO test and cotinine test.

The procedure for this experiment involved prize contingency management for one group and standard care as the control, which the experimenters did not describe (Alessi et al., 2008). The dependent measures in this experiment were the amount of CO expelled from exhaling in parts per million (ppm) and levels of cotinine in saliva as measured in nicotine metabolite per milliliter (ng/ml). In the experimental condition, during CO tests, if the participant blew ≤ 8 ppm (levels indicating abstinence) they were given an opportunity to draw a card from a prize bowl, where cards corresponded to different valued prizes. For each subsequent abstinent result, the number of card draws increased. In the event a positive test was returned or a test was missed, the number of draws was reduced, and the participant was required to show two negative tests to reinstate the previous number of draws, effectively a resetting contingency.

Cotinine was also tested once per week, and tests with results less than 10 ng/ml resulted in bonus draws from the bowls (Alessi et al., 2008). Identical tests were given in the standard care condition, but no contingent prize draws occurred. The procedure involved asking the individual if they were , and one draw per day (non-contingent) was given.   Statistical analysis did not identify statistically significant differences between the incoming characteristics of individuals in the contingency management group and those of the standard care group (Alessi et al., 2008). The authors found reductions in , but not complete cessation per self-report across all participants. At a three-month follow-up, there were three individuals who tested negative for CO, and one at six-month follow-up. However, all of the Cotinine tests came back positive at the six-month follow-up. The data demonstrates none of the participants remained abstinent. Of all missed tests during the study, the majority involved individuals who held jobs off-site. Number of samples submitted also did not differ to a significant degree by group. To begin, there was a positive correlation between not engaging in the behavior of and negative test results (as evidenced by the test results and report) for both groups. In all, prize contingency management was shown to be highly effective in reducing the number of cigarettes smoked within the context of a residential substance abuse clinic during the study, but long-term maintenance of abstinence was not seen.

Dallery and Glenn (2005) conducted a study with four individuals assessing the feasibility of voucher contingency management through the internet. Participants used a computer with a webcam, and CO monitors. In this study, vouchers were contingent upon abstinence in a concurrent multiple baseline across participants with reversal.

Participants logged into the experimenter's website which allowed them to send in videos of CO tests, display data on their cumulative CO levels and voucher earnings, and access a link which allowed for voucher exchange for retailers such as Amazon. The initial baseline required participants to send video of CO monitor results two times per day, which resulted in $5.00 per day. Money was contingent upon submitting samples regardless of CO level.

The next condition involved shaping decreasing CO levels (Dallery & Glenn, 2005). Frequency of in baseline informed the subsequent shaping procedures in the form of progressive reduction. In this shaping condition, each result that met criterion received $3.00. The terminal level of CO established in this condition was one indicating abstinence. For the next ten days, participants entered the abstinence induction condition. The first CO sample that met criterion resulted in a voucher for $3.00, and each subsequent negative sample increased the voucher by $0.25. Every third consecutive negative sample resulted in a bonus $5.00. When a test was failed or missed, the voucher reset to $3.00, and three consecutive negative sessions were required to reset back to the highest voucher value.

The next condition lasted eight days and involved schedule thinning such that individual samples no longer received vouchers or bonuses (Dallery & Glenn, 2005). However, if the fourth and eighth days were negative test results, $5.00 was given. Finally, participants returned to baseline where vouchers were contingent only upon submitting samples. If participants were abstinent for the entire study, they could earn up to $171.50. In addition, a final bonus of $100.00 was given to those individuals who completed the entire study. Through visual analysis of the data, three of the four participants saw a sustained decrease in CO levels relative to baseline throughout the thinning and abstinence induction conditions. One participant maintained low levels following the initial shaping session. The study is socially significant as participants could report their own data using personal computers, and these participants did not need to establish contingency managers.

Dallery et al. (2008) addressed the use of deposit contracts to function as reinforcement, contingent upon abstinence for eight individuals. Four participants deposited $50.00 and could earn an additional $28.80. The reinforcement for the group that did not make a deposit was yoked, such that they could earn a maximum of $78.80. Each participant was provided with a webcam and a CO monitor. Data on CO levels were taken twice per day via webcam video with a minimum of eight hours between each measurement, and results were e-mailed to the experimenter. Participants were able to access a website which displayed voucher earnings and

CO levels across the experiment, and also was used to exchange vouchers at the end of the study. The design of this experiment was an ABCA: baseline, shaping, abstinence induction, and return to baseline. The experiment duration was 24 days, which were consecutive, and vouchers could be earned during the shaping and abstinence induction conditions. Vouchers could then be exchanged at the conclusion of the study.

Baseline involved collecting CO samples two times per day for five days; no programmed consequences were built in (Dallery et al., 2008). In the shaping condition which lasted for four days, vouchers were contingent upon progressively decreasing CO levels relative to baseline measures. By reaching criterion, participants' voucher earnings were $0.50 per result.

In addition, each subsequent negative test resulted in an increase by $0.10. Every three consecutive negative tests resulted in a bonus of $3.00. Failed or positive tests resulted in no voucher and a reset to $0.50 with a requirement of three consecutive negative tests to reinstate the highest earning levels again. The next condition was abstinence induction and this condition lasted ten days. Abstinence induction was identical to the shaping condition in that the voucher schedule remained; however, criterion for vouchers was at 4 ppm. Next, participants moved back to baseline where no programmed consequences occurred upon submitting two results per day.

For seven out of the eight participants, CO levels reduced in shaping and abstinence induction, relative to baseline (Dallery et al., 2008). For these participants, abstinence was identified as four or greater negative consecutive CO samples. Comparing both deposit and no deposit groups, there were no identifiable differences in abstinence (65% vs. 63% negative respectively). The authors found that many samples during baseline were positive, which suggests that this component of self-monitoring did not produce a reduction in in isolation. When the tapering condition was introduced, more samples met criterion for negative results across all groups relative to baseline. The experiment's data suggest that deposit contracts may be a feasible means by which to support a cessation program as individuals effectively provide their own reinforcers by paying what they ultimately earn back. The authors noted that there must be a balance between cost of the deposit, treatment effectiveness, and acceptability of the treatment. They suggested a solution to this would be to use a sliding scale and to explain that the deposit would be less than the individual would otherwise spend on cigarettes.

Dallery et al. (2013) assessed the effects of using a contingency management program through the internet to promote reductions in behavior for 39 individuals. CO monitors were provided for each participant, and laptops with webcams if needed. The maximum amount a participant in this study could earn was $530.00 worth of vouchers, which could be exchanged at any time for gift cards or goods from retailers such as Amazon. As an antecedent measure, all participants in this study were told they should avoid environments where they would be in the immediate area of cigarette smoke or marijuana as this could potentially raise their CO reading. The study allowed participants to contest results of individual tests; this meant that if a positive result was contested and the result both prior and following were negative, vouchers would be awarded. At the same time, for data analysis, the data from the sample remain a positive result.

The design of this experiment involved two treatment groups where vouchers were either contingent upon CO levels, or non-contingent with the voucher amount yoked to a random contingent group participant (Dallery et al., 2013). Participants in the CO group were told the contingency in effect, whereas the non-contingent group were told that they could earn vouchers for submitting CO videos, and that the vouchers would be given or not given on any schedule. Participants used a website that would allow them to submit video of CO test results via webcam. The website also provided data on CO test results, vouchers earned, and messages from the experimenters. A limited hold of eight hours existed such that new results would not be accepted until this time elapsed. Of all 4,774 samples taken through the duration of this study, 39 of them were flagged for having some issue. These issues typically related to technology problems or user input.

The baseline condition duration was three days in which participants were required to submit two video CO samples per day

(Dallery et al., 2013). The next four-day condition involved tapering of CO level criteria for receiving vouchers. Each participant was given reduction goals relative to baseline levels; the terminal criterion for all individuals in this phase was 4 ppm. For each submission that met criterion, a $3.00 voucher was provided. The next 21 days of this study involved abstinence induction. If samples were lower than or equal to 4 ppm, a voucher was provided. The vouchers started at $3.00 and increased by $0.25 for each successive negative result. For every three consecutive negative results, the participant received a bonus $5.00. The authors did not reference to the consequences of a positive result, i.e., whether there was a resetting contingency, or if vouchers were just not provided. The final condition involved 21 days of schedule thinning. Samples were only taken twice per week. Voucher value remained the highest level received in the abstinence induction phase.

The experimenters followed up both 3 months and 6 months after the study was concluded (Dallery et al., 2013). The authors stated that there were few negative CO tests during baseline, and more individuals met criterion during tapering relative to baseline.

Additionally, participants in both conditions showed an increase in negative results in the abstinence induction phase. Of all of the participants in the study, 18% in the contingent group remained abstinent, and 7.7% of the non-contingent group at the three-month follow-ups. Additionally, at the sixmoth follow up, 8% of the contingent CO group and 15.8% of the non-contingent group were abstinent, although the authors said that this disparity was not statistically significant. The results of this study suggest that contingency management over the internet may be effective. An important finding of this study was the high adherence to the submission of video CO monitoring across both the contingent and non-contingent groups. 67% of the contingent CO group and 25% of the non-contingent group gave negative samples across all tests. It is important to note that both groups showed marked reductions in and the results suggest that other factors may influence abstinence. In all, contingency management was slightly more effective than non-contingent vouchers; the effects of feedback, monitoring, and goal setting may have reduced the behavior of across the two groups.

Reynolds et al. (2008) conducted a 30-day study that examined a web based contingency management program with four adolescent individuals. Participants used computers with webcams to send in CO readings three times per day; these readings were required to be separated by at least five hours, and e-mail prompts were sent twice per day. There were five conditions in this ABCDA reversal. Baseline lasted seven days and participants were provided $6.00 per day for submitting their three CO samples as long as they were all separated by at least five hours. The next condition was shaping, and for those four days, participants were given

$3.00 for each negative sample that met criterion to a terminal sample on day four of ≤ 5 ppm. In this condition there were 12 samples, and the maximum amount of money earned was $36.00.

The abstinence induction phase involved providing $2.00 contingent upon the first CO sample of ≤ 5 ppm; each subsequent negative test increased this amount by $0.25 in addition to a $5.00 bonus for every five consecutive test results meeting this criterion (Reynolds et al., 2008). If criterion was not met or a sample was missed, no money was given. The money returned to $2.00 and each subsequent negative increased by $0.25 until three consecutive negative samples were provided, then the amount returned to the highest amount received before reset. In addition, there were several bonuses built in. If the first, second, and third set of 10 samples met all criteria, $10.00 was given, for a total of $30.

Next was thinning, and this condition lasted four days (Reynolds et al., 2008). The criteria for receiving $5.00 per day was that three samples were submitted, and that the final test each day was ≤ 5 ppm. Lastly, participants returned to baseline for five days, and $6.00 per day was provided contingent upon submitting three readings per day. The authors noted that they collected 350 out of 360 potential samples, which was a 97.2% return rate. The authors found that web-based contingency management is a feasible measure to produce cessation in adolescent smokers as evidenced by visual analysis of the data. All participants reduced their CO levels relative to initial baseline, and rates also remained low in return to baseline. The authors mention several potential limitations to external validity; all participants had supportive families and the study was conducted during the school year. In addition, the data did not show a reversal when participants returned to baseline.

Romanowich and Lamb (2010) compared escalating versus deescalating schedules of reinforcement in a contingency management program for cessation. Sixty adults took part in this study. Forty-two of the participants were placed into a large incentive group and the final 18 were placed into a smaller incentive group. Additionally, within these groups, participants were randomly separated into groups of escalating or deescalating schedules of reinforcement. After the intake, each participant was required to provide one CO sample each day during the week for a total of 20 visits. For the first 15 visits, if the participant provided a CO result of < 3 ppm, additional reinforcement was given. For the final five visits, $1.00 was contingent just on providing a sample. For individuals who missed no more than two tests and completed the follow up, a $100 completion bonus was given. For individuals in the escalating larger incentive condition, each negative sample increased the value of the amount given up to a maximum of $100 per sample. A failed sample resulted in not receiving money, but no reset contingency was in place. The descending group of the large incentive condition had a similar contingency except the vouchers reduced in magnitude.

The smaller incentive conditions were identical to the above, except that the amounts were between $1.00 and $32.00 relative to $1.00 and $100.00 (Romanowich & Lamb, 2010). Overall, individuals in the descending groups submitted a higher number of tests that returned negative than individuals in the escalating groups. The authors suggested that descending schedules of reinforcement may promote the highest rates of abstinence relative to escalating schedules for individuals who had no set plans to quit . Additionally, the results were also consistent with prior research in that the higher magnitude of reinforcement produced increasing rates of cessation. However, once abstinence had begun, escalating schedules were more effective at maintaining that abstinence.

Roll et al. (1996) conducted a study assessing the effects of multiple schedules of reinforcement on promoting cessation for 60 individuals. The average number of cigarettes smoked among this group was 26 per day with a range of 10-50. Participants in this study were assigned to three groups: fixed rate of reinforcement, progressive rate of reinforcement, and a yoked control (rates of reinforcement matched with another group).

Participants were required to come to the experimenter's lab three times per day across the fiveday duration of this study. Participants were told to quit the Friday before the start of the study, and abstinence was defined as providing a CO sample of ≤ 11 ppm. For the fixed group, participants were given $9.80 contingent upon negative samples, and there were no bonuses. Participants in the progressive group earned $3.00 contingent upon the first CO reading that met criterion. Each negative sample increased the value by $0.50, and every third negative sample earned a $10.00 bonus. If a result was positive or missed, the money was withheld, the money was reset back to $3.00, and three consecutive negative samples returned back to the prereset value. The yoked group's money was delivered independently of their CO levels and was yoked to members in the progressive group. Each participant was given $50.00 for completing the study.

The results of this study suggested that contingent reinforcement (both fixed and progressive) produced the most abstinence relative to the yoked control (Roll et al., 1996).

Visual analysis of the data show that the progressive group was far less likely to resume relative to the fixed group. Additionally, the progressive schedule also occasioned more participants' behavior of abstinence relative to the fixed schedule. To conclude, this study suggested that contingent payments of a progressive nature, paired with a resetting contingency, may be more effective than contingent fixed or non-contingent payments.

Roll (2005) conducted a study with 22 adolescents who had expressed an interest in quitting . The participants were separated into two groups, which included abstinence or attendance. All participants provided baseline data on CO levels with a CO monitor on two consecutive Fridays prior to the implementation of a four-week contingency management program. The individuals were instructed to continue in the same way they normally would during this period. In intervention, both groups were given information on the dangers of and told to do their best to quit. Each participant gave a daily CO sample and they recorded on a Likert scale their desire and physical need to smoke. In the abstinence group, participants earned $5 vouchers contingent upon providing daily CO samples that met the criterion of < 6 ppm. If they maintained abstinence all week, they received $10.00 for the first, $20.00 for the second, $30.00 for the third, and $40.00 for the fourth. If a sample was positive, the bonuses reset to $10.00. The attendance group design was the same, except that $5.00 vouchers were given contingent upon attending a group session and providing a sample regardless of its result. The findings were that contingency management may be more effective than group meetings as evidenced by analyzing the visual display. Those whose vouchers for cessation were contingent produced lower CO levels, and continued abstinence more often relative to the attendance group.

Roll and Howard (2008) conducted a cessation study for 19 participants in a 5day study comparing two separate interventions: economic gain and economic loss contingent upon abstinence or , respectively. Inclusion criteria included a CO reading $\geq$ 18 ppm, which was indicative of the CO levels of a smoker. Participants were also required to report that they were not currently trying to quit . The study also made use of a depression screening tool (CES-D) as the authors state that may be a product of depression and may exacerbate depressive symptoms. The total potential earnings were $147.50 for both groups.

For each group, a carbon monoxide monitor was used to track levels three times per day in the morning, afternoon, and evening (Roll & Howard, 2008). For the economic gain group, initial negative samples resulted in $3.00, and subsequent negative samples increased by $0.50 with a $10.00 bonus for three consecutive negative samples. A reset contingency was also employed such that a positive sample returned the voucher amount to $3.00. The economic loss intervention was the opposite; the subjects started with a pot of $147.50. Each positive sample resulted in a $3.00 penalty and increased by $0.50 for each subsequent positive sample. If three positive samples were found, an additional $10.00 penalty was given. If there were negative samples, the penalty reduced. For example, if the penalty reached $4.00 and a negative sample was provided, the potential next penalty would return to $3.00.

The results of this study were that participants performed better in the economic gain condition even though the sole difference was the way by which money was delivered (Roll & Howard, 2008). Forty-eight hours of abstinence was met for 90% of the individuals that were in the gain condition and 44% of individuals in the loss condition. No individuals in the gain condition missed consecutive samples and 44% of individuals in the loss condition missed consecutive samples. The data suggest that feedback from providing a positive CO reading could have greater aversive properties when paired with loss of money. The overall findings of this study are that in contingency management procedures, researchers should not focus too much on punishment as it may not keep participants as engaged, nor produce results as positive as reinforcement. When using punishment, researchers need to find a balance between reinforcement and aversive control to ensure treatment fidelity.

Stitzer and Bigelow (1984) conducted an experiment with 23 participants who were separated into two experimental groups. Each participant took part in the baseline session where participants were told to smoke in the same way they normally would. Following week one, participants were told they would be able to earn money contingent upon CO level reduction, and that progressively lower CO levels would result in higher pay amounts. In one group, the pay schedule was changed each day in a randomized fashion such that participants experienced each pay schedule four times. For the other group, the payment schedule was changed weekly such that participants experienced each pay schedule for five consecutive days.

During each session, a breath CO sample was taken, and each participant was given their preferred brand of cigarettes up to the amount they would need until the following session (Stitzer & Bigelow, 1984). Participants tracked when they smoked on a card, and there were five dependent measures: CO levels, cigarettes smoked before session, cigarettes smoked in afternoon, cigarettes smoked in the evening, time since last cigarette, and amount of money earned contingent upon abstinence. The authors reported that the results for daily vs. weekly alternation were virtually the same, as the pay amount was increased, the CO readings decreased, in addition to the number of cigarettes smoked decreasing relative to payment increasing.

Stitzer et al. (1986) conducted a four-week experiment with 34 hospital employees recruited across two hospitals. The experiment began with having the subjects complete a Behavior Attitudes questionnaire, and these questions related to intent to quit . The participants were required to come into a hospital each weekday, at which point they were   provided with cigarettes, and breath CO samples were collected as the baseline. During the second week, the condition changed to a cut-down test, and individuals were given money contingent upon a percentage reduction from baseline in CO readings (e.g., $1.00 for a 30% reduction in CO relative to baseline, and $6.00 for an 80% or more reduction). During week three, participants were told to abstain from and continue for as long as they possibly could, and CO monitoring continued to occur three times per weekday. For those who chose not to participate in this procedure, they returned to baseline in which there was no consequence and they were not told to maintain abstinence.

Of the 34 participants, 23 attempted cessation for the 2-week paid abstinence. During baseline, CO levels were between 30-35 ppm. During cut-down CO levels reduced to 15 ppm for those who initiated a cessation effort compared to 24 ppm for those who did not. Next, during the abstinence condition, abstainers reduced to 5-7 ppm, and non-abstainer's CO readings were at an average of 25 ppm. At follow up three weeks later, four smokers in the abstaining group reported not and had low CO levels, and eight participants from the abstaining group reported 1-104 cigarettes, but their CO readings met abstinent criteria. Lastly, 10 participants reported 81-370 cigarettes, and their CO readings were at non-abstinent criteria. The results of the study suggest that CO monitoring can be an effective method for tracking the behavior of abstinence, and that contingent payment and monitoring may be an effective method by which to promote cessation.

Lamb et al. (2004) assessed the effectiveness of shaping behavior through the use of multiple percentile schedules in a contingency management program for 82 individuals. Use of these percentile schedules individualizes contingencies for reinforcement such that reinforcement is not contingent upon some set CO reading as was the case in all of the above studies. In this study, four schedules were used: 10th, 30th, 50th, and 70th percentile. For example, reinforcement in the 10th percentile schedule on the 10th test would be contingent upon having a lower CO reading than the previous nine. Reinforcement in all of these schedules used an escalating contingency starting with $2.50 and increasing by $0.50 for each result that met criterion. Reset contingencies were in effect; a positive result with CO over criterion required five negative results to return to the highest amount. The findings were that the 70th percentile schedule was the most effective in reducing CO levels and the 10th was least effective, with the 30th and 50th being slightly effective. The intent of percentile schedules in this study was to slowly shape CO levels for difficult-to-treat individuals. When reinforcement occurs frequently for successive reductions, the probability of cessation increases, especially with differential reinforcement. Based on individualized results identified by this study's assessment, percentile schedules like referenced by Lamb et al. (2004) may have been an effective method to systematically shape nicotine use especially when paired with nicotine fading procedures.

Dunn et al. (2008) assessed the effects of voucher-based reinforcement on cessation of participants who were receiving methadone to reduce the effects of opioid dependence. There were

twenty participants in the study, and all had shown an interest in

cessation. All of them reported a minimum of 20 cigarettes a day

within the last year and had been currently receiving methadone for

the previous 30 days. Prior to the study beginning, the participants

completed multiple questionnaires to address their habits

and potential functions of their . The first of these was Fagerstrom Test for Nicotine

Dependence (Heatherton et al., 1991), the Questionnaire of Urges (QSU; Tiffany &

Drobes, 1991), and the Minnesota Nicotine Withdrawal Questionnaire

(MNWQ; Hughes & Hatsukami, 1986). These assessments assess

baseline levels, cravings, and withdrawal, respectively.

These questionnaires were given again at day 14, 30, 60, and 90

(Dunn et al., 2008). Each participant was given $35.00 contingent

upon completing each follow-up, regardless of their status. Each

participant began with a short educational intervention before the

study began. Participants were randomly separated into two groups

receiving contingent and non-contingent vouchers. The study's

duration was 14 days, and during each visit, breath CO and urine

samples were taken, in addition to the participant-reported frequency

of since the prior day, and a daily assessment: brief version of the

QSU referenced above (Tiffany & Drobes, 1991). In the contingent

condition, if the participants met criterion for abstinence ($CO \leq 6$

ppm), vouchers followed, and each member in the non-contingent

condition was yoked to a member of the contingent condition. The first sample that returned at or below this criterion resulted in $9.00, and each subsequent negative sample increased voucher delivery by $1.50. Each sample ≤ 4 ppm resulted in a bonus $10.00 for the first week, and if this criterion was met on day six, it resulted in a $50 bonus. If a sample was missed, vouchers would not be delivered, and the value was reset to $9.00. Following a reset, if two consecutive negative samples occurred, the schedule returned to the pre-reset value. Participants could earn a maximum of $362.50 if they were abstinent for the duration of the study. If a participant missed two consecutive days, they were removed from the study. The non-contingent group's reinforcement was yoked to the contingent groups and they were told that they would get vouchers independent of their cessation effort. If a contingent participant was removed from the study, the yoked status remained, and the non-contingent person received no vouchers.

The results were that participants in the contingent condition returned more negative test results than their non-contingent partners (55% vs 5% respectively; Dunn et al., 2008). In addition, the contingent group also maintained a longer period of abstinence, with fewer reported cigarettes, and lower CO levels overall. The findings of this study were that contingency management may be an effective treatment procedure for promoting cessation among a methadone maintenance population. The authors noted that they used a high magnitude reinforcer as there is a correlation between voucher magnitude and amount of abstinence.

Glenn and Dallery (2007) assessed the effects of voucher reinforcement versus a transdermal nicotine patch for cessation. Effectively, the experimenters assessed the effects of GCR contingent upon abstinence versus an abolishing operation related to nicotine. Fourteen smokers participated in this study and the inclusion criteria was 15 cigarettes or more smoked per day, a history of at least 2 years, that the participant did not live with another individual who smokes, and a desire to quit. Participants were required to send two videos each day showing tests of current CO levels, at intervals of at least 8 hours. Secondly, participants were asked to record the cigarettes they smoked per day, and informed that this number should be honest and would not impact the vouchers given.

All participants received both treatments; half experienced nicotine patches first, and half received vouchers first (Glenn & Dallery, 2007). In baseline, participants earned $5.00, which was contingent just on submitting two CO results each day. In the voucher treatment, vouchers were given contingent upon CO samples ≤ 4 ppm. The first CO test result at this criterion produced a $3.00 voucher with value raising by $0.25 for each successive negative result; a bonus of $5.00 was given for providing three consecutive samples. If a submission was not given or failed, the result was recorded as positive with the voucher returning to $3.00. Three negative samples were required to return to the highest voucher value. The total earnings could be up to $56.25. For patch treatments, participants were given five patches and told to use one per day for the 5-day condition. Lastly, participants returned to baseline.

Visual analysis shows that contingent vouchers reduced the CO levels and the number of reported cigarettes the individual smoked (Glenn & Dallery, 2007). Comparing patches to baseline, the patch did not show significant differences. In voucher treatment, 24% of samples were negative compared to 5% with patches. An important note is that this study did not use a shaping phase reducing the CO ppm gradually. As noted based on results of other studies, voucher-based treatments over the internet may be viable, and the data suggest that patches may not be as effective as this treatment when used with heavy smokers.

GCRs are a socially valid option for the treatment of as evidenced by the robust amount of literature on their effective use. These procedures may specifically train alternative responses by providing substitute or competing reinforcement. Reinforcement does not need to be functionally related to the target behavior. By the same token, access to primary and/or secondary reinforcers contingent upon abstinence may overpower the existing contingencies. For example, money to buy a valuable item in the case of vouchers may be more valuable than access to cigarettes for a week. The literature has suggested high adherence to these types of procedures and identifying the function of the behavior can become unnecessary if the reinforcement is higher in value than access to the reinforcers maintaining . In this study, the effects of voucher-based reinforcement were compared to those of function-based interventions.

The above literature all addresses the behavior of through the use of reinforcement procedures. Vouchers in and of themselves do not address the function of behavior, rather they provide GCR contingent upon engaging in an alternative response to the target behavior. Addressing function is important as a given GCR must be more powerful (e.g., of higher magnitude) than a maintaining variable to promote behavior change. To reiterate, the studies summarized above showed several things: CO monitoring is a viable method by which to track the common dependent variable of CO levels, adherence to submitting CO samples is high amongst populations, contingent reinforcement is far more effective than noncontingent, higher magnitudes of reinforcement produce greater likelihood of cessation, the internet is a viable method for contingency management, and reinforcement should be used over punishment (which is also not function-based). All of this research suggests that CO monitoring is a valid measure by which to assess the dependent variable in this study of CO levels. In addition, salivary cotinine measurement, paired with tracking of the number of cigarettes smoked allowed the primary researcher to track multiple dependent variables correlated to a single behavior.

Environmental Arrangements

Behavior does not occur in isolation; Michael (2004) stipulated that the environment occasions behavior through changes in stimuli rather than static conditions. The environment can be systematically modified to evoke and occasion desired responses and to decrease less desirable behavior. In other words, one must change the environment in order to change the organism's behavior. A modification to the environment could include increasing the response effort required to engage in a particular targeted behavior to decrease the frequency of the behavior itself. Environmental modifications could include escaping or avoiding the environment in which occurs by moving from one location to another. Another option is to increase the response effort of accessing paraphernalia, for example by keeping cigarettes and/or lighters in separate locations. A third option is having paraphernalia under the control of a mediator, where an individual must ask for access to cigarettes when they previously were freely available.

Jason and Liotta (1982) conducted a study assessing the effects of changing an environment to reduce in a university cafeteria. The experimenters attempted to establish stimulus control by placing signs in the cafeteria prompting smokers to engage in the behavior in designated areas. The experimenters' goal was to establish a "non-" section. The dependent variables in this study were tracked each day between 12:00 and 12:50 pm; these variables were the number of people and the number of seconds smoked in each quadrant. The initial baseline was conducted for the first 10 days. In Condition 1, which lasted

16 days, signs stating "Non- for Health and Comfort of Patrons" were placed in the cafeteria. Following a 5-day return to baseline, in Condition 2, sign prompting returned in addition to a maximum of two verbal prompts indicating the sign. In Condition 2, experimenters monitored degree of compliance with the prompt(s). Condition 1 then returned for eight days, followed again by Condition 2 for five days.

In the two baseline sessions, the range of total duration per 50-min testing interval was 39 and 50 min across an average of 7.7 individuals; that is, at least one individual must have been for the duration counter to continue (Jason & Liotta, 1982). In Condition 1, the reduced to 26 min across an average of 5.3 individuals. In Condition 2, the average was 6.2 minutes across an average of 1.6 individuals. When assessing compliance, 54% of participants completely complied, 27% reached partial criterion, and 19% did not. The combination of signs and prompting were the most successful intervention. However, prompting was not addressed in isolation, and that could have led to the decrease of behavior relative to the signs and prompting. In addition, individual participants' ongoing compliance with the non- requirements were not assessed. Following the study, the cafeteria maintained the non- section, and a worker offered to prompt individuals to not smoke in the particular non- area. Environmental arrangements, at the antecedent level may be function-based in the sense that they may abolish the value of the consequence of a behavior. At the same time, a competing response or incompatible response may or may not be function-based when considering matched stimuli. Punishment is an environmental arrangement; however, it occurs as a consequence, and is not function-based.

Environmental arrangements are specific actions an individual may take to change the environment, which in turn may produce the desired behavior change. Simple interventions such as changing access to paraphernalia are easy and low-cost steps an individual can take.

Nicotine Fading

The concept of nicotine fading is to track an individual's baseline levels of nicotine and over time, systematically reduce that individual's dependence on nicotine by fading out to more stringent abstinent criterion. Foxx and Brown (1979) compared four cessation programs across 44 participants. These programs included nicotine fading, self-monitoring, nicotine fading and self-monitoring in combination, and the American Cancer Society program. Before the study began, the participants attended an orientation where they completed a questionnaire related to their behavior and watched a film by the American Cancer Society. Each participant provided a $15.00 deposit. Half that deposit would be delivered when treatment concluded, and the other half at follow-up. The initial half of the deposit was contingent upon following the smoker's contract, attending each weekly session, providing significant other's contact information, keeping daily records of , and submitting cigarette butts from each pack smoked. These participants were told the collection of cigarette butts related to assessing the weight of tobacco left; this was deception, as the experimenters were assessing if the participants were correctly fading to less nicotine.

In the nicotine fading group, the goal was to slowly reduce the amount of nicotine consumed by changing brands to those with progressively less nicotine (Foxx & Brown, 1979). In week four, the goal was to quit altogether. In the self-monitoring group, participants were told to track their intake of nicotine/tar on two separate charts. The combined nicotine fading/selfmonitoring group included both treatments. Finally, group four received an American Cancer Society program which the authors modified. The American Cancer Society program involved support meetings during which participants provided tips and tricks to help each other remain abstinent. In each condition of the experiment, groups came together for an hour each week for five consecutive weeks. The meeting period(s) were used to discuss successes and failures related to each treatment package. Following the experiment, participants were contacted at several intervals for up to 18 months following the study to assess average number of cigarettes smoked, brand smoked, and number of abstinent days.

If participants were not successful, they were given the treatment procedure with the best results during the study (Foxx & Brown, 1979). There were not any participants in the selfmonitoring group that became abstinent. At the six-month follow up, the nicotine fading/selfmonitoring group was 50% abstinent, and no other group had higher abstinence than 10%. At 18 months, 40% of the nicotine fading/self-monitoring group was still abstinent. All but one participant in the nicotine fading/self-monitoring group who had not quit had switched to a lower tar/nicotine brand. In all, the nicotine fading/self-monitoring group was the most successful in decreasing nicotine/tar and achieving abstinence. The next most successful treatments in order were nicotine fading, the American Cancer Society program, and then self-monitoring. An important consideration is that these procedures did not involve aversive control, such that limitations of these procedures were avoided. Antecedent measures may be successful in decreasing the amount of nicotine/tar someone consumes, and in promoting long term abstinence.

Malott et al. (1984) conducted a multiple baseline across behaviors to assess the effects of co-worker social support on cessation at a worksite. There were two conditions, one with controlled , and the other with controlled plus partner support. Twentyfour participants were recruited and they provided a $15.00 deposit, which would be returned if the participants attended treatment and follow up. The group averaged 24 cigarettes per day at the onset of the study, were an average of 34 years of age, and averaged 16 years of . The dependent variables were nicotine content, total number of cigarettes smoked, and percentage of each cigarette smoked. Participants measured their behavior for one week, which functioned as a baseline. For the first condition, controlled , participants met for 6 weekly meetings which were about 50 min in duration and included steps by which to systematically reduce nicotine content through changing brands, reducing the number of cigarettes per day, or reduce the percentage of a cigarette that would be smoked. Additionally, progress was discussed at each of these meetings, and individual goals were set. These participants were then asked if they would prefer to reduce further, quit completely, or maintain current levels, and given booklets related on how to do this.

The second condition was controlled /partner support; it included everything above, except that the individual met with a partner each day and used the Partner's Controlled Manual (Malott et al., 1984). The dependent variables were self-report of frequency and topography of , weight of cigarette butts, CO levels, and responses to questionnaires. Data in the visual display were aggregated across participants. For the controlled condition, initial included 0.7 mgs of nicotine content vs. 0.8 mgs for partner support, between 20 and 24 cigarettes each day vs. 24 cigarettes per day for partner support, and

85% of each cigarette smoked for both groups. With the introduction

of tracking nicotine content, weight decreased to 0.4 mgs and then to

0.25 mgs vs. 0.45 mgs and then to 0.4 mgs for partner support. When

the 25% reduction in number of cigarettes per day was introduced, the

average number smoked reduced to 17 for both conditions, and when

the second reduction occurred, behavior decreased to approximately

10-13 cigarettes per day vs. 13 cigarettes per day for partner support.

Next, the intervention of reduction of percentage of cigarettes smoked

was implemented; percentage smoked reduced to 70% for both

conditions, and when the 50% reduction was introduced, this further

reduced to 60% for both conditions. The findings were that co-worker

supports were not effective in increasing treatment efficacy and there

were minimal differences in outcomes across both groups. Of the

individuals who quit , all were still abstinent at follow up. In addition,

of the individuals who did not become abstinent, all exhibited lower

levels across all dependent variables.

Nicotine fading as an antecedent intervention can be function-

based if nicotine is determined to be the reinforcement maintaining

and the intervention decreases behavior when nicotine is abolished as

a reinforcer (Malott et al., 1984). Nicotine fading appears to be a socially significant treatment as it is a readily self-selected intervention. Purchasing nicotine patches or gradually reducing the number of cigarettes smoked is a way for an individual to change their own behavior without the need for someone else to mediate. However, while this treatment addresses an assumed function of nicotine, it may not be a generally effective treatment. With this in mind, while this intervention may be preferred, it may not be effective for all individuals.

Extinction

Extinction, defined by Cooper et al. (2020), is "the discontinuing of reinforcement of a previously reinforced behavior (i.e., responses is no longer produce reinforcement); the primary effect is a decrease in the frequency of the behavior until it reaches a pre-reinforced level or ultimately ceases to occur" (p. 457). There has been a dearth of research on extinction as a treatment for in the *Journal of Applied Behavior Analysis*, and that is most likely a product of the fact that a functional assessment does not currently exist, which would prevent functional application of extinction. Extinction could conceivably be an effective treatment for , if the treatment corresponds to the functional variables maintaining the behavior. If it does not, the treatment may be contraindicated. This study employed extinction components such as informing individuals in a person's life not to provide attention contingent upon if it is determined that the behavior was maintained by attention, or to not allow escape from work contingent upon is the behavior maintained by escape from specific demands. Nicotinemaintained could have been placed on extinction if some form of device that was topographically similar and produced every consequence with the exception of nicotine. However, in general, treatment packages focused on proactive approaches to reinforce more acceptable alternative behaviors, while also abolishing the value of other types of maintaining reinforcement.

In terms of the social validity of extinction procedures, it may not be possible for these treatments to be easily self-administered; the client or participant would need to arrange someone else to place their targeted behavior on extinction, and this may be done incorrectly or intermittently. Lerman and Iwata (1996) discussed how extinction procedures will be less effective when intermittent schedules of reinforcement are utilized, as this would increase resistance to extinction. In other words, an extinction procedure will be most effective when the functional consequence no longer ever follows the target behavior. Additionally, extinction procedures may not be selected or readily adhered to in the first place. Hanley et al. (2005) suggested that in some cases, punishment may be preferred to extinction procedures. In their study, participants were given to option to select treatment packages, and a punishment procedure for the targeted response was selected over extinction procedures. In the end, extinction is an effective procedure, but may not be effective for self-managed behavior change in the case of .

Research Question(s)

This research compared the effects of function-based treatment packages developed with the input of participants on self-reported frequency of , levels of CO, and levels of salivary cotinine to those of voucher-based reinforcement. Additionally, adherence to each treatment package (i.e., procedural fidelity) was assessed. Based on the assumed function-based treatment packages, the validity of an indirect functional assessment in identifying the function of behavior is discussed.

Chapter 3: Study I Pilot

The purpose of the pilot study survey was to ask open-ended questions to identify variables that occurred before, during, and after individuals smoked, in addition to reasons why they self-reported engaging in this behavior. Every individual's behavior is unique and there may be innumerable different reasons why each person smokes, e.g., unique environments, different people, variables before/during/after many activities, and certain stimuli. These data were used to inform possible perspectives on questions to ask that were pertinent to each category (i.e., participants individually gave statements that would suggest certain function(s)).

Method

Participants and Experimental Setting

Ten participants were recruited for this study and participated anonymously (i.e., no names or signatures were collected) via Facebook posts, Craigslist posts, flyers at The Chicago School, and through an email to The Chicago School students, all including a link to Survey Monkey with embedded consent (Appendix B & C). Participants ranged in age from 27-51 with a mean age of 36.3.

The original posting on Craigslist Fort Lauderdale, FL (community-general) did not result in any replies within the first two weeks. At that time, the Craigslist ad was extended to Chicago, IL. In addition, the primary investigator posted the link and explanation of the study on Facebook and requested for others to also share the post. The link was re-shared several times to garner more responses both across Craigslist and Facebook during the month when the postings expired. Facebook produced all responses, with Craigslist not recruiting any responses (across Chicago and Fort Lauderdale).

There were no pre-screening procedures and participation in the pilot study was completely voluntary. If the participants met the self-reported criterion of currently engaging in behavior, they had the ability to participate in the pilot study. Participants had the ability to provide online consent in lieu of formal written consent by advancing from the informed consent screen to the survey itself. The procedures above were conducted 100% online, through SurveyMonkey.

Materials

The pilot study questionnaire (Appendix D) consisted of 16 questions; four were closedended, 10 were open-ended, and one was a Likert scale chart with 24 responses possible that indicated how often individuals smoked per hour in a typical day. At the end, a statement was included that "if you wish to enter in the raffle, please provide your e-mail." The survey took

approximately 30 min to complete.

The first page of the SurveyMonkey provided information about participant response, time to complete the survey, directions for providing email (for raffle), discussion of confidentiality (as no identifiable information would be connected to responses). The first page of the Survey Monkey fulfilled the function of the consent process.

The first question was the only demographic information collected: "what is your age?", and this was paired with the third question "how many years have you been ?" The second question in this survey was "how many cigarettes do you smoke in a day?" This 24-hour span was separated by hour-long intervals and provided six options related to the question of "on a typical day, how many cigarettes do you have within each hour?" The possible responses to this question were 0, 1, 2, 3, 4, 5+, and N/A: Sleeping.

> The fourth question in this survey was the first to address function. The question was:

"what are some of the reasons you smoke?" The next three questions were "what are you typically doing (before/while/after) a cigarette?" The next question was "what are some of the locations you smoke?" The next question asked, "who are the groups of people you smoke with?" The next question continued along the same lines as the previous: "Do you smoke more often alone, with strangers, with friends, with co-workers, colleagues or with family?"

The next three questions were "are there any emotions/feelings you experience

(before/when/after) you smoke?" The final primary survey question relating to cigarette use was

"have you tried to quit previously? If so, what have you tried?" The optional response related to entering in one's e-mail to have their information placed into a raffle.

Procedures

In order to create the pilot study SurveyMonkey, the primary researcher compiled potential environmental variables affecting the behavior of and input them into an Excel document. The pilot study survey was created based on these potential variables. The pilot study flyer was distributed online and via print in the Experimental Setting section.

Once the primary and secondary investigators deemed there were enough responses to suggest a variety of environmental events that could affect the behavior of across individuals, the survey was closed. At the closing of the survey, the primary investigator compared the number of reported cigarettes in questions two and sixteen across participants to assess reliability of measures via self-report across questions which effectively ask the same thing, just in different modalities. Secondly, the remaining questions were aggregated to populate statistics on average age of participants, average years of , the remaining responses were then categorized to see if any common trends had arisen, e.g., common reports of reasons an individual smokes and common antecedents, activities, or consequences across all individuals. Once all of the self-report data were compared, they were transferred to an Excel document and connected with potential functions.

Following the survey, if participants provided their e-mail address they were entered into a raffle for the opportunity to win one of ten Amazon online gift cards, which was conducted 3 months after survey's results were coded.

Results

Survey results are shown in (Appendix E). Participants reported between 1-20 cigarettes per day with a median across these individuals being 5. Average years of ranged from 4-36 years with the median being 17.5 years. Common reported reasons and antecedent events for included alcohol, social situations, addiction, pleasure, relaxation, breaks, transitions, sexual situations, and stress inoculation. Almost all participants reported satisfaction and relief when they were . The majority of participants reported engaging in behavior in the presence of others. In response to the clarifying question of who do these individuals smoke most often around, half reported alone, and half reported with friends/family. Locations of included outside, bars, restaurants, home, work, vehicles, and at parties. These participants reported emotions of craving, anger, frustration, anxiety, guilt, joy, and boredom prior to . Participants reported previous self-administered treatments such as leaving cigarettes at home, Chantix/Wellbutrin, nicotine patches, gum, going cold turkey, and electronic cigarettes/vaping devices.

Discussion

Each participant presumably had a unique learning history regarding and responses to survey questions showed that there may be many different functions for across people (i.e., not one consistent function). Participant self-reports can be categorized into broad functions of social positive reinforcement, social negative reinforcement, and automatic reinforcement (e.g., access to nicotine or escape from withdrawal symptoms). Other indicated functions included, removal or avoidance of some form of aversive stimuli (such as tasks at work, transitions, school, people, etc.), all indicated the social negative umbrella of escape. Additionally, access to specific individuals or their reactions were categorized under the umbrella of attention. Tangible reinforcement such as food, alcohol, and activities were also categorized under the category of social positive reinforcement.

Reports of the above tangible examples may indicate that is multiply maintained based on context. When individuals drink alcohol, in many cases they may be in the presence of other complementary reinforcers such as other individuals, music, dancing, food, or a myriad of other variables that presumably have been paired with in the past. At the same time, the fact that many individuals reported social interaction to be collateral to could lend itself to a common social positive function for in the sense that meaningful social interaction can occur both during and after the behavior of .

Since there were reports across many potential functions, and these participants all attempted different interventions, these results support conclusions that a once size fits all treatment for would have limited effectiveness. Non function based interventions could explain why these individuals were not successful in long term cessation, even if they were previously briefly successful.

Chapter 4: Study II

Assessment Creation

The indirect functional assessment used in this study was created by first establishing four broad categories of function: social positive, social negative, automatic positive, and automatic negative. These reflected functional categories as first described for the use of functional assessment by Iwata et al. (1994). A test for potential function requires multiple questions for repeated measures. Responses were tied to a Likert scale ranging from strongly disagree (-2) to strongly agree (2). Agreement was scored on the y-axis above zero and disagreement was scored on the y-axis below zero. A running list of six categories for each potential function (e.g., Attention, Escape, Automatic Positive, Automatic Negative) was created based on the pilot study assessment results and the primary investigator's review of the literature (Appendix F). Each sub-category included six specific questions for a total of one hundred fortyfour across all four functions. Additionally, by each sub-category including an even number questions, the potential for undifferentiated results would be limited (as the pilot suggested that the behavior of may be multiply controlled). Next, a scoring guide (Appendix G) was created to include a value, the question number, scoring, and each individual function. Attention included the sub-categories of: Friends/Family, Others Request, With Others, Draw Attention, New People, and Non-Approval. Escape included the sub-categories of: Break from

Tasks, Remove Situation, Remove People, Remove Boredom, Remove Transit, and Avoid Task.

Automatic Positive included the sub-categories of: Buzz/Jump Start, Smoke/Embers, Cigarette Burn, Cigarette Smell, Flicking/Ashing, and Cigarette Taste. Automatic Negative included the sub-categories of: Reduce Stress, Reduce Appetite, Reduce Withdrawal, Remove Pain, Remove

Thoughts, and Avoid Withdrawal.

Questions related to potential social positive functions needed to include several scenarios as related to context: the people involved, if positive or negative attention was delivered, proximity of people possibly providing reinforcement, and the stimuli that may have evoked/occasioned the response. To begin, may either occur when a person is alone or with someone, with someone they know, or with strangers. Questions must also involve the type of reinforcement provided: positive attention (e.g., socialization), or negative (e.g., disapproval). Other questions involved how the behavior was evoked/occasioned. Additionally, questions included if the individual smokes with others, if another person initiated the behavior, or if the individual initiated in the absence of people. Questions related to potential social negative functions included the same considerations noted above and were broken down by escape (stimulus terminated), and avoidance (stimulus averted). Potential variables that were considered included tasks, people, and activities/transition from activities. Tasks were also separated into escape (e.g., to get a break from work and/or school) and avoidance (e.g., to avoid writing a paper). Regarding the variable of specific people, an individual may smoke to escape or avoid people, but may also remove themselves from an aversive situation (e.g., to avoid or get out of uncomfortable situations). Lastly, there were instances where tasks are not present, and that could function as aversive stimulation in the case of transitions (as referenced in the pilot

e.g., driving, activities ending, and transitions to new activities). Several questions were added to address these situations (e.g., I smoke when I'm driving and I smoke between activities).

Potential functions related to automatic positive reinforcement may be related to stimuli that may or may not be present to others in the environment but involve an individual's senses. Visual senses involve anything an individual may see (e.g., the smoke and/or embers). Tactile senses involve anything an individual may feel (e.g., the burn of the cigarette smoke in one's lungs). Sometimes this stimulation is indistinguishable in the case of visual stimulation that may also be tactile in nature (e.g., flicking/ashing cigarettes). Olfactory senses involve smell, and gustatory senses involve taste. Lastly, engaging in the behavior of often produces a "high" or buzz which may be described in many ways (e.g., tingling fingers, warmness, relaxed feeling, etc.).

Stimuli associated with functions related to automatic negative reinforcement are also not readily visible to another observer. In some cases, this stimulation's removal may be inferred as it relates to collateral responses and public accompaniments. To begin, many individuals in the pilot referenced cigarette as a form of stress inoculation (e.g., responses including "I smoke to reduce stress/anxiety" and "I smoke to clear my head"). Cigarette was also reported as an appetite suppressant. Automatic negative reinforcement within a functional assessment like the Questions About Behavior Function (QABF) (Paclawskyj et al., 2000) can also relate to pain/stimulation removal. While this particular stimulation was not mentioned by participants in the pilot study, pain reduction (automatic negative reinforcement) is still addressed in assessment. Lastly, continual cigarette at regular intervals throughout the day may indicate an individual is maintaining their nicotine levels; which could be related to positive reinforcement in the form of access to nicotine or negative reinforcement in the form of avoidance of withdrawal symptoms, and these questions were included in assessment.

Chapter 5: Methodology

Participants and Recruitment

Participants were recruited online via a flyer posted to Facebook (Appendix H). All ads included contact information for the primary researcher to pre-screen participants (Appendix I). To be included, participants were required to be age 21 or older. Participants were required to currently identify as consuming cigarettes daily and have an interest in cessation. An additional note was that these tests are sensitive to marijuana (CO levels) and that if the participant smokes marijuana they were excluded. Participants were also required to have the ability to hold their breath for at least 15 seconds. The pre-screening process did not require participants to provide identifiable information, and this information was either collected via a phone call or HIPAA compliant video chat.

Exclusion criterion were as follows: participants under the age of twenty-one, identification of being a non-smoker, reporting consumption of marijuana, and inability to hold one's breath for more than 15 seconds.

Settings

Participants were in contact with the primary investigator through e-mail, Zoom, and in person. With this in mind, the experimental setting was the participant's own environments (work, school, home, in transit, etc.).

Materials

The primary materials for this research included an indirect functional assessment and scoring guide (Appendix F & G), informed consent forms (Appendix J), a pre-assessment selfreport screening & demographic questionnaire (Appendix K), a script for running the functional assessment (Appendix L), assessment PowerPoint slides (Appendix M) a sample of what results may look like (Appendix N), a treatment selection handout (Appendix O), a

Micro+ ™ basic Smokerlyzer® carbon monoxide reader (Appendix P), cotinine tests (Appendix Q), tally counters (2) (Appendix R), a research process map (Appendix S), Treatment Integrity/Process Checklist (Appendix T), a dependent variable IOA form (Appendix U), a voucher based progressive reinforcement key (Appendix V), a participant responsibility & voucher delivery key (Appendix W), materials introduction sheet (Appendix X), email follow-up templates (Appendix Y- EE), a participant treatment integrity sample form (Appendix FF), an email debriefing (Appendix GG), a maintenance follow-up email (Appendix HH), and a social validity survey (Appendix II).

Dependent Variables and Response Measurement

The primary dependent variables in this study were CO levels, salivary cotinine readings, and participants' self-report of cigarettes smoked. Cotinine levels are higher in smokers than non-smokers and have been used in previous studies to assess cessation, in addition to standard CO monitoring. CO was tracked three times per day to be consistent with the half-life of carbon monoxide. Additionally, a cotinine reading was be taken twice per week as an additional measure. Lastly, the half-life of cotinine is approximately 16-19 hours as reported by Jarvis et al. (1988) as opposed to CO having a half-life of approximately 8 hours. CO readings required multiple tests per day to address the efficacy of treatment; (e.g., one test per day would only allow assessment of CO levels from several hours prior to the test). Additionally, cotinine is a supplemental measure of tobacco use as nicotine metabolizes in the liver regardless of delivery method (e.g., chewing tobacco, hookah, vaping, snuff, etc.) and any access to nicotine would have been reflected by the test.

Participants had the ability to report their CO and Cotinine test results remotely and have them delivered directly to the researcher without the barriers associated with in person meetings. In addition, participants were also asked on a daily basis to report on the frequency of cigarettes smoked. Concurrently, participants completed a checklist regarding adherence to their treatment plan. No negative consequences were provided related to study non-adherence in the baseline or function based phases of the study as vouchers were given contingent upon submission (regardless of results). These adherence values were recorded daily. In the voucher based condition, the programmed consequence from the investigator was a resetting contingency for positive or missed tests, and participants were asked to take these tests truthfully. Additionally, HIPAA compliant video chat was intermittently utilized for CO test(s) to address IOA, in addition a secondary researcher was able to verify the permanent products (photograph of cotinine test(s)/CO levels.

Dependent Variable IOA

Dependent variable IOA in this study was measured by utilizing Trial by Trial IOA, which is identified by Cooper et al. (2020, p. 116.) as "the number of trials or items agreed, divided by the total number of trials or items, times 100." The IOA methodology measured the percentage of agreement between researchers (e.g. if both primary and secondary researchers record a value of 10, this would be total agreement on the step (100%), whereas if there is any disparity between values reported by primary and secondary researcher, the value on that step became (0%)). IOA was calculated using the Dependent Variable IOA form provided in

Appendix U. The number of steps differed across participants based on the total study duration.

IOA was 100% across all participants: Participant 1 (350/350), Participant 2 (420/420),

Participant 3 (420/420), Participant 4 (105/105) (Table 1).
Table 1

Dependent Variable IOA Results

	Primary Researcher	Research Assistant	Total Agreement	Count
Participant 1	350 Data Points	350 Data Points	100%	
Participant 2	420 Data Points	420 Data Points	100%	
Participant 3	420 Data Points	420 Data Points	100%	
Participant 4	105 Data Points	105 Data Points	100%	

Note. Dependent Variable IOA reflective of the total number of data points for each participant

Experimental Design & Condition Sequence

The experimental design for this study included conditions ABAC with debriefing and a one-month follow-up after any terminal condition. A process map flow chart is available in (Appendix S). Each participant began in baseline (A), once steady state responding was reached (2-4 weeks) the participant received a function-based treatment package (B). If treatment failed to be successful (Condition B), the participant returned to the baseline (A) until steady state responding was reached (2 weeks), and subsequently advanced to a voucher based reinforcement condition (C) (4 weeks). All participants received a debriefing on conditions and they were provided with supplemental evidence based cessation materials regardless of when the study concluded.

Pre-Experimental Assessment(s)

Prior to the experiment beginning, the participant was provided with all relevant prescreening materials, self-report questionnaire (Appendix K), informed consent (Appendix J), and the functional assessment (Appendix F) was provided to determine hypothesized function and an evidence-based intervention. Pre-Experimental results

Questions from assessment were presented individually in a

PowerPoint (Quasi-Randomized for each participant) with a scoring

key at the top listing the likert scale. Additionally, the primary

researcher split the assessment into thirds, such that a five-minute

break was available for every 48 questions presented, to decrease

fatigue or address nicotine withdrawal, although no participant used

their break opportunity.

Coding Assessment Results

The quasi-randomized questionnaire (i.e., no function is

repeated in order) was coded with four primary values (Strongly

Disagree = (-2), Disagree = (-1), Agree = (1), and Strongly Agree =

(2). Additionally, a Not Applicable (X) option was provided.

Negative values were added together to specify level of disagreement

within the function sub-category, and the positive values were added

together to specify the level of agreement within the function

subcategory. Effectively, this coding provided the researcher the

ability to identify potentially maintaining variables within and across

sub categories, and also correspondence of questions (e.g., are the

questions reliable and valid in the sense that the participant answers them all in the same way, and do the questions correspond to the listed function/sub-category) The primary researcher entered values into Excel and Excel was programmed to code and graph results automatically.

Statement Agreement

Scores of +9 to +12 indicated participant report that this function sub-category is strongly correlated with , such that when relevant MOs and SDs are in place, there is a very high probability of occurring (66-100%).

Values of +4 to +8 indicated participant report that this function sub-category is semicorrelated with , such that when relevant MOs and SDs are in place, there is a moderate probability of occurring (33-65%).

Values of 0 to +3 indicated participant report that this function sub-category is rarelycorrelated with , such that when relevant MOs and SDs are in place, there is a low probability of occurring (0-32%).

Statement Disagreement

Values beginning at -1 and advancing to -12 indicate progressively stronger participant report of an inverse relationship between and these function sub-categories. Effectively, is rarely evoked or reinforced given these environmental conditions.

Cumulative Results

Total values of 54-72 (across all sub-categories within a function) strongly indicated participant report of a maintaining variable of .

Total values of 24-53 moderately indicated participant report of a maintaining variable behavior.

Total values of 0-23 indicated minimal participant report of a maintaining variable of .

Baseline

Baseline tracked multiple variables (e.g., self-report of cigarettes consumed, CO levels, and salivary cotinine pass/fail). During this time, the participants were instructed to continue to smoke at the same levels (and not attempt intervention at this point) and tracked their cigarette consumption, provided two salivary cotinine measurements each week, and tracked CO levels three times each day (Morning, Afternoon, & Evening). Participants were given access to all electronic materials required for treatment and data collection.

Introduction to baseline and weekly email cadence are demonstrated in Appendix Y & Z. Participants were also provided $.25 in vouchers per submitted CO reading (max of 3 per day) and $1 for each salivary cotinine test (max of 2 per week), which was delivered at the conclusion of each respective phase. Once steady state responding was identified or a maximum reached (4 weeks), the participant advanced to the function based treatment condition. A return to baseline occurred in the event function based treatment was ineffective (e.g., the trend in reduction did not allow for timely achievement of the goal), utilizing the same steps from above. The return to baseline condition continued until steady state responding was reached or a maximum of x weeks if steady state responding was not observed. Following the return to baseline, the participant advanced to the voucher based treatment condition.

Function Based Treatment

The transition email from baseline to function based treatment was demonstrated in (Appendix AA). The function based treatment condition consisted of a behavior plan created from the functional assessment and shaped by participant preference (to address social validity). During this condition, the participant tracked their cigarette consumption, collected two salivary cotinine measurements each week, and tracked CO levels three times each day. The primary researcher collected data on a daily basis and assessed treatment effectiveness. Weekly email cadence was demonstrated in Appendix BB. HIPAA compliant video chat was utilized (once per phase) for CO level IOA and functioned as additional control to prompt ethical responding and create a learning history of submitting truthful measurement. Participants were given 24hrs of notice and had the ability to select from the Morning, Afternoon, or Evening readings. Similar to baseline, participants were also given $.25 in vouchers per submitted CO reading (max of 3 per day) and $1 for each salivary cotinine test (max of 2 per week) as a reinforcement contingency, which was delivered at the conclusion of each phase. To remain in the function based treatment package, the participant was required to reduce their cigarette consumption (from baseline) by 25% by week two, 50% by week four, 75% by week five, and 100% by week six, at which point, the study concluded. If the participant was within a 5% margin of error, they still advanced to the next phase as data points are averaged across the full phase interval and the frequency of behavior took time to come under the stimulus control of the current condition. For participants that did not meet the pre-established continuation criterion, they returned to baseline, and subsequently advanced to a voucher-based reinforcement system (see email communication to participants regarding this phase change in Appendix CC & DD). Across any phase, if a participant became unresponsive for (3) days, as verified through visual analysis of the raw data, they were sent an intermediary email (Appendix EE), outside of the weekly email check-in and after (2) of these follow-ups, the participant(s) were removed from the study.

Selection of a Function Based Treatment

Based on the results of the indirect functional assessment and variables reported to be correlated with during baseline data collection, the primary investigator met with the participant to review the potential function of their and the recommended treatment methods based on that function. Reviewing these treatment suggestions allowed the primary researcher to solicit participant's input in selecting their own treatment package, which strengthened the social validity/effectiveness as described in Olympia et al. (1994) regarding student selected performance goals being more effective than arbitrarily selected goals

Categories of behavior function described below with potential options of intervention selection. As an additional note, participants agreed to not utilize nicotine replacement in the form of nicotine patches, nicotine gum, or vaping devices in the function based condition. No participant's assessment results suggested utilizing as a tool for physical pain attenuation, therefore, none were removed from the study.

Collateral to Social Attention

The contingency between and social attention is broken. Social attention is already reinforcing, and may function as an additional collateral reinforcer. Family, friends, and colleagues may occasion or evoke the behavior, so consider that paraphernalia should be removed from environments where social attention may be presented. Additionally, increasing the quality and quantity of social attention in other environments will be necessary when limiting access to the secondary reinforcer of .

Collateral to Escape from an Environment

Ensure the individual may still escape the environment (without). An individual may still take a break with the same exact topography, instead they may engage in a competing or incompatible response (e.g., lollypop, toothpick, etc.), while still removing themselves from that environment. The intervention is especially true of removing oneself from environments that serve alcohol.

Collateral to Task Delay/Escape

Modify tasks to reduce aversive properties, and/or build in reinforcing stimuli contingent upon task completion/non avoidance. High p is an option: start by completing the least probable task, and move to progressively less aversive (i.e., more reinforcing) tasks. Building in additional reinforcers is imperative as the task(s) themselves are inherently aversive. Additionally, a checklist may be utilized to check off the completion of each item.

Collateral to Escape from Transition

Alter the aversive properties of the transition from one task to the next. Is a behavior that keeps your hands busy? Is a behavior to kill time between tasks? Is a scheduled activity when a task ends?

as a Stimulant

Match the stimulating effects of nicotine. The individual may choose to select a stimulus that would produce a stimulating effect such as caffeine (i.e., coffee, tea, caffeinated soda, and/or pre-workout).

Byproducts as Reinforcement

Ensure individual would maintain access to several matched stimuli without the harmful/addictive byproducts. The individual may choose to maintain access to others without engaging in the specific topography (e.g., visual and olfactory access to smoke). Tactile stimuli may also be easily matched (e.g., something to hold), however, taste/burn of cigarettes are not easily matched without engaging in the behavior of , and incompatible/competing responses may be most preferable such as chewing gum, toothpicks, candy, drinking coffee/tea, etc.

as Stress Inoculation

Individual selects other coping mechanisms for stress inoculation. Additionally, the individual may choose to select competing/incompatible responses to engage in when they feel stressed/anxious.

to Avoid Withdrawal

Individual will systematically fade access to nicotine. These interventions may include:

systematic fading of the number of cigarettes consumed each day or utilizing a cold turkey method and stopping consuming cigarettes on day one.

as an Appetite Suppressant

Focus on appetite reduction in the absence of a cigarette. Interventions may include consuming more liquid, or consuming smaller portions over a longer period of time, chewing bites for extended periods of time, or ensuring consistent access to snacks.

as a Tool for Pain Attenuation

Please seek medical consultation.

Voucher-Based Reinforcement

The voucher-based reinforcement condition was utilized in the event the function-based intervention failed to be successful in promoting reasonable reductions in as identified by the participant's titration level. For the scenario where a voucher-based reinforcement procedure was needed, the participant first returned to baseline (2-4 weeks) and, advanced to the 28 day voucher-based reinforcement procedure. Weekly email cadence was provided (Appendix DD). Participants were told that cessation would result in contingent vouchers in (GCR) and that they would be able to design any intervention they see fit. To be consistent with the literature on maximal effectiveness for voucher-based treatment, this procedure employed contingent payments of a progressive nature, paired with a resetting contingency as in Roll et al., 1996. Similar to the function-based condition, participants were still be eligible to receive vouchers contingent upon submitting CO readings and cotinine tests regularly (regardless of reading) and this condition also included the HIPAA compliant video chat for IOA. abstinence was identified as a CO reading of ≤ 4 ppm. Cessation vouchers were only presented if the participant was under this threshold. The first negative CO test as identified by a reading of ≤ 4 ppm resulted in $.25, and each submitted negative test increased this value by $.05. If a participant failed to submit a CO reading or was over the ≤ 4 ppm threshold, no vouchers were given, and the participant's maximum voucher amount was returned to $.25 until the participant presented three consecutive negative tests in a row. On the third consecutive negative test, the participant advanced to the next voucher level higher than their previous maximum (.e.g., a failed test resulted in: 0, .25, .25, then increased). Each participant had the ability to earn up to $165.55 in vouchers contingent upon negative readings (84 opportunities), an additional $22.50 contingent upon general submission of readings (84 opportunities), and $8 contingent upon submission of salivary cotinine readings (8 opportunities). The voucher-based reinforcement condition ended after a set 28 days.

Treatment Integrity for Participants

Treatment integrity was addressed by the participants completing a daily checklist regarding submission of data collection on the number of cigarettes consumed per day, CO tests per day, cotinine test submission, and behavior plan adherence in the function based phase(s) (Appendix FF) and Treatment Integrity Results in Figure 1-4. These adherence values were reported individually and aggregated for a total daily score (e.g., 65/70 steps).

Participant 1's treatment integrity (Figure 1) in baseline (4 weeks) was 87%, 50%, 37%, & 59%. Treatment integrity in the function based, 25% reduction phase, (2 weeks) was 82% and 75%. Treatment integrity in the function based, 50% reduction phase, (2 weeks) was 68% and 73%. Treatment integrity in the function based, 75% reduction phase, (1 week) was 77%. Treatment integrity in the function based, 100% reduction phase, (1 week) was 71%. Participant 1 reported 100% treatment fidelity (behavior plan adherence) as related to following the treatment protocol: Escape (42/42) and Automatic Negative (42/42) on the

dates of 8/23/2021 – 10-3-2021

   Participant 2's treatment integrity (Figure 2) in baseline (2
   weeks) was 73% and 93%,

Treatment integrity in the function based, 25% reduction phase, (2
weeks) was 93% and 93%.
Treatment integrity in the function based, 50% reduction phase, (2

weeks) was 73% and 89%. Treatment integrity in the return to

baseline phase, (2 weeks) was 77% & 93%. Treatment integrity in the

voucher based, phase, (4 weeks) was 70%, 87%, 80%, & 67%.

Participant 2 reported 100% treatment fidelity (behavior plan

adherence) in his titration protocol: Environmental Arrangements

(28/28) and Attention (28/28) on the dates of 8/2/2021 – 8-29-

2021.

   Participant 3's treatment integrity (Figure 3) in baseline (2 weeks)
                                      was 100% and 100%,

Treatment integrity in the function based, 25% reduction phase, (2
weeks) was 98% and 93%.

Treatment integrity in the function based, 50% reduction phase, (2

weeks) was 97% and 93%. Treatment integrity in the return to

baseline phase, (2 weeks) was 80% & 97%. Treatment integrity in the

voucher based, phase, (4 weeks) was 93%, 90%, 73%, & 77%.

Participant 3 reported 100% treatment fidelity (behavior plan adherence) in his titration protocol: Escape (28/28) and Automatic

Negative (28/28) on the dates of 12/20/2021 – 1-16-2022.

Participant 4's treatment integrity (Figure 4) in baseline (2

weeks) was 100% and 87%, Treatment integrity in the function based,

25% reduction phase, (1 week) was 73%. Participant 4 reported 71%

treatment fidelity (behavior plan adherence) in his titration protocol:

Automatic

Negative (5/7) on the dates of 1/17/2021 – 1-23-2022.

Treatment Integrity for Researcher and TI IOA

The researcher completed a treatment integrity checklist

detailing each experimental step (Appendix T). Researcher Treatment

integrity was 100% for all participants (Table 2). Treatment integrity

was addressed by a secondary researcher who also completed the

treatment integrity checklist (Appendix T) regarding the primary

researcher's delivery of permanent products and completed steps.

These adherence values were aggregated for a total score (e.g., 65/70

steps) and included 100% of all steps for all participants.

Table 2

Treatment Integrity for Researcher and TI IOA

	Primary Researcher	Research Assistant	Total Count Agreement

Participant 1	40/40 Steps	40/40	100%
Participant 2	51/51 Steps	51/51	100%
Participant 3	51/51 Steps	51/51	100%
Participant 4	21/21 Steps	21/21	100%

Note. This table illustrates the Researcher Treatment Integrity results and IOA results.

Debriefing & Maintenance Fading Plan

Participants were provided with a debriefing email (Appendix GG) depicting the purpose of the study, a brief overview of evidence based practices for cessation, why treatment was selected, and tools to identify naturally occurring reinforcing (e.g., reductions in insurance referral costs, long term benefits, etc.). In addition, they were also given the results of their functional assessment with information on how treatment was selected. Debriefing occurred in the event a participant decided to drop out of the study (within any condition). Additionally, if a participant was successful in cessation within the function-based treatment they would receive the debriefing as well. In any scenario where the participant received the voucher-based condition, a debriefing followed that phase too regardless of treatment success.

Maintenance Probe

One month following the completion of the study, the primary researcher contacted the participant and provided a maintenance probe and social validity questionnaire (Appendix HH & II), Completion of this questionnaire, regardless of success with cessation, resulted in a

$10 voucher. Participant 4 did not complete this follow up.

Voucher Delivery

The vouchers were delivered to the participant via email (Amazon Gift Card) within 48 hours of their individual completion of respective phases. Additionally, the participants that responded to the maintenance probe questionnaire received an additional $10 voucher that was delivered the same day.

Chapter 6: Results

Documented results may be found here: Voucher Delivery Results (Table 3),

Participant Pre-Assessment Self-Report Questionnaire & Demographics, Raw Data, and

Maintenance Probe/Social Validity Questionnaire: Participant 1: (Table 4-6), Participant 2:

(Table 7-9), Participant 3: (Table 10-12), Participant 4: (13-14)

Table 3

Voucher Delivery Results

	Baseline Earned	Follow-Up	Follow-Up Earned	Follow-Up Max
Participant 1	$8.00	$10	$6.00	$10
Participant 2	$8.00	$10	$4.00	$10
Participant 3	$10.50	$10		N/A

Baseline Max	Function Based Earned	Function Based Max	Baseline Earned	Baseline Max	Voucher Based Earned	Voucher Based Max
$21.00	$15.25	$31.50	X	N/A	X	N/A
$8.00	$9.00	$12.00				
$10.50	$15.75	$21.00	$8.25	$10.50	$62.55	$165.55
$4.00	$5.00	$8.00	$4.00	$4.00	$4.00	$8.00
$10.50	$19.00	$21.00	$8.75	$10.50	$2.50	$165.55
$4.00	$8.00	$8.00	$4.00	$4.00	$8.00	$8.00
$10.50	$3.75	$5.25	X	N/A	X	N/A
$4.00	$2.00	$2.00				

Participant 3 $4.00

Participant 4	$9.75	X
	$3.00	

Note. This table illustrates the total voucher delivery across participants.

Participant 1

Participant 1 was a 38-year-old Asian/Japanese male whom reported working full-time and holding a Master's degree. He reported that COVID affected his personal (intimate) relationship and resulted in starting again. There was no concern in financial uncertainty affecting his ability to access cigarettes through the duration of the study. He reported that anxiety/stress was the primary function in his and his reason for wanting to quit was for his overall health (Table 4).

Table 4

Participant 1: Pre-Assessment Self-Report Questionnaire & Demographics

1) Name: XXX
2) Age: 38
3) Gender: Male
4) Race/ethnicity: Asian/Japanese
5) Highest level of education you've completed: Masters
6) Employment status: Employed, Full Time 7) Contact Email: XXX
   8) Address:
XXXX
XXX
XXX

COVID-19 Impact
9) How has your behavior been affected by COVID-19?

Relationship changes and COVID re-started

10) Has your frequency of changed given social distancing?
Yes

11) Has an income change prompted you to quit ?
No, no employment changes

12) Will financial uncertainty as a result of COVID-19 affect your access to cigarettes?
Possible

13) Will financial uncertainty as a result of COVID-19 affect your access to internet?
Very unlikely

Rationale

14) Why do you think you continue to smoke?
Anxiety, stress

15) What prompts you to want to quit now? Health, not a solution for anxiety

Note. This table displays Participant 1's Pre-Assessment Self-Report Questionnaire &

Demographics.

Participant 1's assessment results are displayed in Figure #5.

Participant 1's assessment result in the Attention function are as

follows: Friends/Family (+1 Agree, -5 Disagree), Other's

Request (+1 Agree, -5 Disagree), With Others (+1 Agree, -5 Disagree), Draw Attention, (+0

Agree, -6 Disagree), New People (+0 Agree, -5 Disagree), Non-Approval (+0 Agree, -6

Disagree). Participant 1's assessment results in the Escape function are as follows: Break from

Tasks (+2 Agree, -3 Disagree), Remove Situation (+6 Agree, -0 Disagree), Remove People (+4

Agree, -1 Disagree), Remove Boredom, (+1 Agree, -5 Disagree), Remove Transit (+4 Agree, -2

Disagree), Avoid Task (+0 Agree, -6 Disagree). Participant 1's assessment results in the

Automatic Positive function are as follows: Buzz/Jump Start (+2 Agree, -3 Disagree), Smoke/Embers (+2 Agree, -4 Disagree), Cigarette Burn (+0 Agree, -7 Disagree), Cigarette

Smell, (+1 Agree, -6 Disagree), Flicking/Ashing (+0 Agree, -6 Disagree), Cigarette Taste (+0

Agree, -6 Disagree). Participant 1's assessment results in the

Automatic Negative function are as follows: Reduce Stress (+6

Agree, -0 Disagree), Reduce Appetite (+1 Agree, -4 Disagree),

Reduce Withdrawal (+1 Agree, -5 Disagree), Remove Pain, (+0

Agree, -6 Disagree), Remove Thoughts (+6 Agree, -1 Disagree),

Avoid Withdrawal (+2 Agree, -2 Disagree).

Figure #9 displays cessation data for Participant 1 & raw data

(Table 5). The right hand Y axis specifies the number of cigarettes

consumed per day.(line graph with circle data points), the left hand Y

axis specifies the carbon monoxide levels throuought the day

(morning, afternoon, and evening) (bar graph). These CO levels are

coded by gradient from light gray (morning), medium gray

(afternoon), and dark gray (evening). Additionally, a pass fail

measure existed for cotinine at the level of a smoker and non-smoker.

These measures are at the top of the graph and identified by an open square (pass-non-smoker), and a closed square (fail-smoker). All participant graphs followed this same format.

In initial baseline (4 weeks), Participant 1 consumed 45 cigarettes, submitted 32/84 CO tests (ranging between 1 and 7ppm), and 6/8 cotinine tests (5 at criterion of a smoker and one at the criterion of a non-smoker).

In the function based, 25% reduction phase, (2 weeks), Participant 1 consumed 14 cigarettes (69% reduction), submitted 24/42 CO tests (ranging between 1 and 4ppm), and 2/4 cotinine tests (2 at the criterion of a smoker and none at the criterion of a non-smoker).

In the function based, 50% reduction phase, (2 weeks), Participant 1 consumed 0 cigarettes (100% reduction), submitted 17/42 CO tests (ranging between 1 and 2ppm), and 3/4 cotinine tests (0 at the criterion of a smoker and 3 at the criterion of a non-smoker).

In the function based, 75% reduction phase, (1 week), participant 1 consumed 0 cigarettes (100% reduction), submitted 11/21 CO tests (ranging between 1 and 2ppm), and 2/2 cotinine tests (0 at the criterion of a smoker and 2 at the criterion of a non-smoker).

In the function based, 100% reduction phase, (1 week), participant 1 consumed 1 cigarette (99.98% reduction), submitted 8/21 CO tests (ranging between 1 and 2ppm), and 2/2 cotinine tests (0 at the criterion of a smoker and 2 at the criterion of a non-smoker).

In initial Baseline (4 weeks), the data were of a low level, decreasing trend, and low variability (0-4 cigarettes). When advancing to the function based, 25% reduction phase (2 weeks), data were of a low level, decreasing trend, and low variability (0-2 cigarettes). In the function based, 50% reduction phase (2 weeks), data were of a low level, stable trend, and no variability (0 cigarettes). In the function based, 75% reduction phase (1 week), data were of a low level, stable trend, and no variability (0 cigarettes). In the function based, 100% reduction phase (1 week), data were of a low level, stable trend, and almost no variability (1 cigarette).

Participant 1's earnings (Table 3) were as follows for CO tests and Cotinine Tests: Baseline ($8.00/$6.00), function based ($15.25/$9.00), follow up ($10), for a grand total of $48.25.

At one-month follow-up (Table 6), Participant 1 self-reported that they still remained a non-smoker. He identified his success to setting goals and keeping records although he reported that he is not perfect at this practice. Participant 1 also reported that he enjoyed seeing his progress and feeling better. When it comes to factors he did not enjoy about the study was the additional stress regarding submission of tests. As it relates to his behavior plan, he felt that he played an active role in its selection, guided by the primary researcher. From a social significance standpoint, the report that the participant felt they took an active role in treatment selection, may have promoted a greater level of success than a one size fits all intervention.

Table 5

Participant 1: Raw Data

			Participant Entered				Researcher Entered										
Condition: Baseline	Date	Day	#Cigarettes	Escape	ActoutNeg.	TI1	CLOevel 1	%COvHbel	CLOevel 2	%COvHbel	CLOevel 3	%COvHbel	Cotinine	Above/Below	Vouchers	Total
	7/26/21	Monday	3	N/A	100%	1	Yes	3 1.11	Yes	3 1.11	Yes	2 0.95	Yes	Above	$$$$$ 10.20 .2 05 0	$$$ 0.00 . . 2 2 55	$ 1.75

Condition: Baseline

Date	Day	#Cigarettes	Escape	AutoN	TI	CO Level 1 (submitted)	CO Level 1	%COHb	CO Level 2 (submitted)	CO Level 2	%COHb	CO Level 3 (submitted)	CO Level 3	%COHb	Cotinine	Above/Below	Voucher	Voucher	Voucher	Voucher	Total
7/27/21	Tuesday	3			100%	Yes	2	0.95	No			Yes	4	1.27	No	Select	$-	$0.25	$-	$0.25	**$0.50**
7/28/21	Wednesday	3			100%	Yes	2	0.95	No			Yes	4	1.27	No	Select	$-	$0.25	$-	$0.25	**$0.50**
7/29/21	Thursday	3			100%	Yes	2	0.95	Yes	4	1.27	No			Yes	Above	$1.00	$0.25	$0.25	$-	**$1.50**
7/30/21	Friday	4			100%	Yes	3	1.11	Yes	7	1.75	Yes	6	1.59	No	Select	$-	$0.25	$0.25	$0.25	**$0.75**
7/31/21	Saturday	2			100%	No			Yes	2	0.95	Yes	6	1.59	No	Select	$-	$-	$0.25	$0.25	**$0.50**
8/1/21	Sunday	3			100%	Yes	3	1.11	Yes	7	1.75	Yes	4	1.27	No	Select	$-	$0.25	$0.25	$0.25	**$0.75**

Printed column headers (as shown at foot of table): Date | Day | #Cigarettes | Escape | AutoN | TI | CO Level 1 | %COHb | CO Level 2 | %COHb | CO Level 3 | %COHb | Cotinine | Above/Below | Vouchers | Total

Date	Day	#Cigarettes	Escape	Aut	TI1	CLOe1	%C	CLOe2	%C	CLOe3	%C	Cotinine	Above/Below	Vhoe	Total
				e.g.											
8/2/21	Monday	4			100%	Yes 4	1.27	Yes 4	1.27	Yes 7	1.75	Yes	Above	$1.00 $0.25 $0.25 $0.25	$1.75
8/3/21	Tuesday	1			100%	No		No		No		No	Select	$- $- $- $-	$-
8/4/21	Wednesday	2			100%	No		No		No		No	Select	$- $- $- $-	$-
8/5/21	Thursday	2	N/A		100%	No		No		No		No	Select	$- $- $- $-	$-
8/6/21	Friday	1			100%	No		No		No		No	Select	$- $- $- $-	$-
8/7/21	Saturday	3			100%	No		No		Yes 3	1.11	No	Select	$- $- $- $0.25	$0.25
8/8/21	Sunday	2			100%	Yes 2	0.95	No		Yes 4	1.27	Yes	Above	$1.00 $0.25 $- $0.25	$1.50

Date	Day	#Cigarettes	Escape	Aut	CO1 vel	CO1 OHb	CO2 vel	CO2 OHb	CO3 vel	CO3 OHb	Cotinine	Above/Below	Vhoe	Total
8/9/21	Monday	2		100%	Yes 2	0.95	No		No		No	Select	$- $0.25 $- $-	$0.25
8/10/21	Tuesday	1		100%	No		Yes 2	0.95	No		No	Select	$- $- $0.25 $-	$0.25
8/11/21	Wednesday	2	N/A	100%	Yes 1	0.79	No		No		No	Select	$- $0.25 $- $-	$0.25
8/12/21	Thursday	1		100%	Yes 2	0.95	No		No		No	Select	$- $0.25 $- $-	$0.25
8/13/21	Friday	0		100%	No		No		No		No	Select	$- $- $- $-	$-
8/14/21	Saturday	0		100%	No		No		No		No	Select	$- $- $- $-	$-
8/15/21	Sunday	0		100%	No		No		No		No	Select	$- $- $- $-	$-

			o N e g.		v el	O Hb	v el	O Hb	v el	O Hb					ur cs		
8/16/21	Monday			0%	No		No		No		Yes	Below	$1.00	$-	$-	$-	$1.00
8/17/21	Tuesday			0%	No		No		No		No	Select	$-	$-	$-	$-	$-
8/18/21	Wednesday			0%	No		No		No		No	Select	$-	$-	$-	$-	$-
8/19/21	Thursday	1	N/A	100%	No		No		No		No	Select	$-	$-	$-	$-	$-
8/20/21	Friday	1		100%	Yes	1	0.79	Yes	2	0.95	No		Yes	Above	$1.00	$0.25	$0.25	$-	$1.50
8/21/21	Saturday	1		100%	Yes	1	0.79	No		No		No	Select	$-	$0.25	$-	$-	$0.25
8/22/21	Sunday	0		100%	No		Yes	1	0.79	Yes	1	0.79	No	Above	$-	$-	$0.25	$0.25	$0.50

Total Phase   **$14.00**

Condition/Functionhood — Date	Day	#Cigarettes	Escape	Auto Neg.	TI	CL Oe 1	vel	%COHb	CL Oe 2	vel	%COHb	CL Oe 3	vel	%COHb	Cotinine	Above/Below	Vhoeurcs				Total
8/23/21	Monday	1	Yes	Yes	100%	Yes	1	0.79	Yes	3	1.11	Yes	1	0.79	No	Select	$-.25	$0.25	$0.25	$0.25	$0.75
8/24/21	Tuesday	2	Yes	Yes	100%	Yes	3	1.11	Yes	1	0.79	Yes	4	1.27	Yes	Above	$1.00	$0.25	$0.25	$0.25	$1.75
8/25/21	Wednesday	1	Yes	Yes	100%	Yes	2	0.95	Yes	2	0.95	Yes	2	0.95	No	Select	$-.25	$0.25	$0.25	$0.25	$0.75
8/26/21	Thursday	1	Yes	Yes	100%	Yes	2	0.95	Yes	2	0.95	No			No	Select	$-.25	$0.25	$0.25	$-	$0.50

Date	Day	#Cigarettes	Escape	Auto Neg.	TI 1	CO Level 1	%COHb	CO Level 2	%COHb	CO Level 3	%COHb	Contine	Above/Below	V hours	Total
8/27/21	Friday	2	Yes	Yes	100%	No		Yes 4	1.27	No		No	Select	$- $- $0.25 $-	$0.25
8/28/21	Saturday	1	Yes	Yes	100%	Yes 4	1.27	No		No		No	Select	$- $0.25 $- $-	$0.25
8/29/21	Sunday	1	Yes	Yes	100%	No		No		Yes 1	0.79	No	Select	$- $- $- $0.25	$0.25
8/30/21	Monday	1	Yes	Yes	100%	Yes 3	1.11	Yes 2	0.95	Yes 1	0.79	No	Select	$- $0.25 $0.25 $0.25	$0.75
8/31/21	Tuesday	0	Yes	Yes	100%	No		Yes 2	0.95	Yes 2	0.95	Yes	Above	$1.00 $- $0.25 $0.25	$1.50
9/1/21	Wednesday	1	Yes	Yes	100%	No		Yes 1	0.95	No		No	Select	$- $- $0.25 $-	$0.25

9/2/21	Thursday	1	Yes	Yes	100%	No			Yes	2	0.95	Yes	2	0.95	No	Select	$-	$-	$0.25	$0.25	**$0.50**
9/3/21	Friday	1	Yes	Yes	100%	Yes	2	0.95	Yes	3	1.11	Yes	3	1.11	No	Select	$-	$0.25	$0.25	$0.25	**$0.75**
9/4/21	Saturday	1	Yes	Yes	100%	No			No			No			No	Select	$-	$-	$-	$-	$-
9/5/21	Sunday	0	Yes	Yes	100%	No			No			No			No	Select	$-	$-	$-	$-	$-

Condition: FunctionBased

Date	Day	#Cigarettes	Escape	Auto Neg.	TI	CO1	Level	%COHb	CO2	Level	%COHb	CO3	Level	%COHb	Cotinine	Above/Below	Vouchers				Total
9/6/21	Monday	0	Yes	Yes	100%	No			No			No			No	Select	$-	$-	$-	$-	$-
9/7/21	Tuesday	0	Yes	Yes	100%	Yes	1	0.79	No			Yes	1	0.79	No	Select	$-	$0.25	$-	$0.25	**$0.50**

Condition: Function based

Date	Day	#Cigarettes	Escape	Auto Neg.	TI	CLOe1	Level	%COHb	CLOe2	Level	%COHb	CLOe3	Level	%COHb	Cotinine	Above/Below	Vhoeurcs				Total
9/8/21	Wednesday	0	Yes	Yes	100%	Yes	1	0.79	No			No			Yes	Below	$1.00	$0.25	-	-	**$1.25**
9/9/21	Thursday	0	Yes	Yes	100%	Yes	2	0.95	Yes	2	0.95	Yes	1	0.79	No	Select	-$0.25	$0.25	$0.00	$0.00	**$0.75**
9/10/21	Friday	0	Yes	Yes	100%	Yes	1	0.79	Yes	1	0.79	No			No	Select	-$0.25	$0.25	$0.00	-	**$0.50**
9/11/21	Saturday	0	Yes	Yes	100%	No			No			No			No	Select	-	-	-	-	**-**
9/12/21	Sunday	0	Yes	Yes	100%	No			No			No			No	Select	-	-	-	-	**-**
9/13/21	Monday	0	Yes	Yes	100%	Yes	1	0.79	No			Yes	1	0.79	Yes	Below	$1.00	$0.25	-	$0.25	**$1.50**

Date	Day	#Cigarettes	Escapet	Auto Neg.	TI1	CLOe1	vel	%COHb	CLOe2	vel	%COHb	CLOe3	vel	%COHb	Cotinine	Above/Below	Vouchers				Total
9/14/21	Tuesday	0	Yes	Yes	100%	Yes	1	0.79	No			Yes	1	0.79	No	Select	$-	$0.25	$-	$0.25	**$0.50**
9/15/21	Wednesday	0	Yes	Yes	100%	No			No			Yes	1	0.79	No	Select	$-	$-	$-	$0.25	**$0.25**
9/16/21	Thursday	0	Yes	Yes	100%	Yes	1	0.79	Yes	1	0.79	No			Yes	Below	$1.00	$0.25	$0.25	$-	**$1.50**
9/17/21	Friday	0	Yes	Yes	100%	No			No			Yes	1	0.79	No	Select	$-	$-	$-	$0.25	**$0.25**
9/18/21	Saturday	0	Yes	Yes	100%	Yes	1	0.79	No			No			No	Select	$-	$0.25	$-	$-	**$0.25**
9/19/21	Sunday	0	Yes	Yes	100%	No			No			No			No	Select	$-	$-	$-	$-	**$-**

Condition:Functional and

143

9/20/21	Monday	0	Yes	Yes	100%	No			Yes	2	0.95	Yes	1	0.79	Yes	Below	$1.00	$-	$0.25	$0.25	$1.50
9/21/21	Tuesday	0	Yes	Yes	100%	No			Yes	1	0.79	Yes	1	0.79	No	Select	$-	$-	$0.25	$0.25	$0.50
9/22/21	Wednesday	0	Yes	Yes	100%	No			Yes	1	0.79	Yes	1	0.79	No	Select	$-	$-	$0.25	$0.25	$0.50
9/23/21	Thursday	0	Yes	Yes	100%	Yes	1	0.79	Yes	2	0.95	No			Yes	Below	$1.00	$0.25	$0.25	$-	$1.50
9/24/21	Friday	0	Yes	Yes	100%	Yes	1	0.79	Yes	1	0.79	No			No	Select	$-	$0.25	$0.25	$-	$0.50
9/25/21	Saturday	0	Yes	Yes	100%	Yes	1	0.79	No			No			No	Select	$-	$0.25	$-	$-	$0.25
9/26/21	Sunday	0	Yes	Yes	100%	No			No			No			No	Select	$-	$-	$-	$-	$-

Date	Day	#Cigarettes	Escape pet	Auto Neg.	ATI	CLOe1	CO Level	%COHb	CLOe2	CO Level	%COHb	CLOe3	CO Level	%COHb	Cotinine	Above/Below	Vouchers	Vouchers	Vouchers	Vouchers	Total
9/27/21	Monday	0	Yes	Yes	100%	Yes	1	0.79	Yes	2	0.95	Yes	1	0.79	Yes	Below	$1.00	$0.25	$0.25	$0.25	$1.75
9/28/21	Tuesday	0	Yes	Yes	0%	No			Yes	2	0.95	No			No	Select	$-	$-	$0.25	$-	$0.25
9/29/21	Wednesday	0	Yes	Yes	0%	No			Yes	1	0.79	No			Yes	Below	$1.00	$-	$0.25	$-	$1.25
9/30/21	Thursday	0	Yes	Yes	0%	Yes	1	0.79	Yes	1	0.79	No			No	Select	$-	$0.25	$0.25	$-	$0.50
10/1/21	Friday	0	Yes	Yes	0%	No			Yes	1	0.79	No			No	Select	$-	$-	$0.25	$-	$0.25
10/2/21	Saturday	1	Yes	Yes	0%	No			No			No			No	Select	$-	$-	$-	$-	$-

	10/3/21	Sunday	0	Yes	Yes	0%	No		No		No		No	Select	$-	$-	$-	$-	$-
Total Phase																			$24.25

Note. This table illustrates participant 1's study raw data & voucher earnings.

Table 6

Participant 1: Maintenance Probe/Social Validity Questionnaire

At this time, are you currently ?
No
If no: What have you found to be contributing to your success?
-I thrive by keeping records & watching the goal especially financially & makes me kept in check
If yes: What have you found to be contributing factors in starting or continuing to smoke? Do you find the current study to be useful (Function based cessation), if so, why, and if not, why not?
-I think so, for me (I'm not perfect at keeping records), you have to be really committed to do it, and the time requirements, and travel makes it difficult. What did you enjoy about this study? **-Seeing progress & feeling better** What did you not enjoy about this study?
-Missing tests, adds additional stress (I have to do this…I have to squeeze it in) What changes would you suggest for research in the future?
-I didn't think about it
Did you feel that you played an active role in selecting your own intervention?

-Yes

Note. This table illustrates a Maintenance Probe/Social Validity Questionnaire used to follow up on Participant 1's behavior following the conclusion of the experiment.

Participant 2

Participant 2 was a 51-year-old White male who reported working full-time and had completed high school. He reported that COVID had not affected his life as related to . There was no concern in financial uncertainty affecting his ability to access cigarettes through the duration of the study. He reported that the primary function of is as a habit and his reason for wanting to quit was that he has wanted to quit for a long time, thinks is stinky, and alienates you from others (Table 7).

Table 7

Participant 2: Pre-Assessment Self-Report Questionnaire & Demographics

1) Name: XXX
2) Age: 51

3) Gender: Male
4) Race/ethnicity: White
5) Highest level of education you've completed: High School
6) Employment status: Employed, full time 7) Contact Email: XXX
    8) Address:
XXX
XXX
XXX

COVID-19 Impact
9) How has your behavior been affected by COVID-19?
No Change
10) Has your frequency of changed given social distancing?
No Change
11) Has an income change prompted you to quit ? No
12) Will financial uncertainty as a result of COVID-19 affect your
    access to cigarettes? No
13) Will financial uncertainty as a result of COVID-19 affect your
    access to internet? No

 Rationale
14) Why do you think you continue to smoke?
 is a habit
15) What prompts you to want to quit now?
Wanted to quit for a long time, and participant thinks is "stinky" and
alienates you from others

Note. This table displays Participant 2's Pre-Assessment Self-Report
Questionnaire &

Demographics.

Participant 2's assessment results are displayed in Figure #6.

Participant 2's assessment result in the Attention function are as

follows: Friends/Family (+4 Agree, -3 Disagree), Other's Request (+6

Agree, -0 Disagree), With Others (+7 Agree, -0 Disagree), Draw

Attention, (+0

Agree, -12 Disagree), New People (+7 Agree, -0 Disagree), Non-Approval (+0 Agree, -12

Disagree). Participant 2's assessment results in the Escape function are as follows: Break from

Tasks (+0 Agree, -8 Disagree), Remove Situation (+0 Agree, -12 Disagree), Remove People (+0

Agree, -9 Disagree), Remove Boredom, (+1 Agree, -5 Disagree), Remove Transit (+0 Agree, -12

Disagree), Avoid Task (+0 Agree, -12 Disagree). Participant 2's assessment results in the

Automatic Positive function are as follows: Buzz/Jump Start (+0 Agree, -9 Disagree),

Smoke/Embers (+0 Agree, -12 Disagree), Cigarette Burn (+0 Agree, -12 Disagree), Cigarette

Smell, (+0 Agree, -11 Disagree), Flicking/Ashing (+0 Agree, -10 Disagree), Cigarette Taste (+0

Agree, -7 Disagree). Participant 2's assessment results in the

Automatic Negative function are as follows: Reduce Stress (+0

Agree, -4 Disagree), Reduce Appetite (+0 Agree, -12 Disagree),

Reduce Withdrawal (+0 Agree, -9 Disagree), Remove Pain, (+0

Agree, -12 Disagree), Remove Thoughts (+2 Agree, -6 Disagree),

Avoid Withdrawal (+0 Agree, -9 Disagree).

Figure #10 displays cessation data for Participant 2 & raw data (Table 8). No features of this graph are different from the graph for participant 1. In initial baseline (2 weeks), Participant 2 consumed 24 cigarettes, submitted 32/42 CO tests (ranging between 1 and 17ppm), and 4/4 cotinine tests (3 at criterion of a smoker and 1 at the criterion of a non-smoker). Note that for this participant, the baseline data from week 2 were utilized for criterion establishment as to not mask the high rates of behavior through aggregation of a low week (week 1), and a high week (week 2).

In the function based, 25% reduction phase, (2 weeks), Participant 2 consumed 34 cigarettes (30% reduction), submitted 36/42 CO tests (ranging between 1 and 8ppm), and 3/4 cotinine tests (1 at the criterion of a smoker and 2 at the criterion of a non-smoker).

In the function based, 50% reduction phase, (2 weeks), Participant 2 consumed 45 cigarettes (6% reduction), submitted 27/42 CO tests (ranging between 1 and 9 ppm), and 2/4 cotinine tests (1 at the criterion of a smoker and 1 at the criterion of a non-smoker).

In the return to baseline, (2 weeks), participant 2 consumed 26 cigarettes (46% reduction), submitted 33/42 CO tests (ranging between 1 and 2ppm), and 4/4 cotinine tests (1 at the criterion of a smoker and 3 at the criterion of a non-smoker).

In the voucher based phase, (4 weeks), Participant 2 consumed 32 cigarettes (66% reduction), submitted 61/84 CO tests (ranging between 1 and 4ppm), and 4/8 cotinine tests (0 at the criterion of a smoker and 4 at the criterion of a non-smoker).

In initial Baseline (2 weeks), the data were of a moderate level, increasing trend, and high variability (0-22 cigarettes). When advancing to the function based, 25% reduction phase (2 weeks), data were of a moderate level, increasing trend, and high variability (0-19 cigarettes). In the function based, 50% reduction phase (2 weeks), data were of a moderate level, decreasing trend, and high variability (0-19 cigarettes). In the return to Baseline, (2 weeks), data were of a moderate level, decreasing trend, and high variability (0-13 cigarettes). In the Voucher Based phase (4 weeks), the first two weeks were of a moderate level, decreasing trend and moderate variability (0-9 cigarettes), the second two weeks were of a moderate level, increasing trend, and moderate variability (0-11 cigarettes).

Participant 2's earnings (Table 3) were as follows for CO tests and Cotinine Tests: Baseline ($8.00/$4.00), function based

($15.75/$5.00), Baseline 2 ($8.25/$4.00), Voucher based ($62.55/$4.00) follow up ($10), for a grand total of $111.55.

At one-month follow-up (Table 9), Participant 2 self-reported that they still continued to smoke but the amount of was significantly less than before the study began. He identified he continues to smoke related to habit, but not a physical or mental "thing", but the behavior is mostly correlated with drinking. Participant 2 also reported that he thought the study was useful in that he now thinks about each cigarette, and to regularly score the monitor, which created a game to do better than the last test. Additionally, the participant reported that the e-mail reminders helped in being more successful and needing to actively count the number of cigarettes he consumes. Participant 3 reported that he thought the equipment was cool, and how easy the charting was, in addition to his graphs at the end of the study. As for things Participant 2 did not enjoy about the study is that he felt guilty when he forgot to submit tests, given that the researcher is not a stranger to him. As for future changes, Participant 2 commented that he wishes the assessment specifically asked about alcohol consumption as being collateral to , and this is discussed later. When it came to if the participant felt they played an active role in developing their treatment, Participant 2 reported that they played the "primary role" which may lend itself, from a social significance standpoint to the level of effectiveness of his treatment.

Table 8

Participant 2: Raw Data

Condition:Baseline	Date	Day	#Cigarettes	Environment	Social	TI1	CLOevel	%COHb	CLOe2vel	%COHB	CLOe3vel	%COHB	Cotinine	Above/Below	Vouchers	Total
	7/19/21	Monday	0			100%	Yes 3	1.11	No		Yes 1	0.79	No	Select	$-.25 $0.25 $-.25 $0.00	$0.50
	7/20/21	Tuesday	2			100%	Yes 2	0.95	No		Yes 3	1.11	No	Select	$-.25 $0.25 $-.25 $0.00	$0.50
	7/21/21	Wednesday	0	N/A		100%	Yes 2	0.95	No		Yes 1	0.79	No	Select	$-.25 $0.25 $-.25 $0.00	$0.50
	7/22/21	Thursday	0			100%	Yes 2	0.95	No		Yes 1	0.79	Yes	Below	$1.00 $0.25 $-.25 $0.00	$1.50

Date	Day	#Cigarettes	Environment	Social	TI	CLOe1 Level	%COHb	CLOe2 Level	%COHB	CLOe3 Level	%COHB	Cotinine	Above/Below	Vouchers				Total
7/23/21	Friday	0			100%	Yes	2	0.95	No		No			No	Select	$-	$0.25	$-	$-	$0.25
7/24/21	Saturday	0			100%	Yes	2	0.95	No		No			Yes	Below	$1.00	$0.25	$-	$-	$1.25
7/25/21	Sunday	0			100%	Yes	2	0.95	Yes	3	1.11	Yes	2	0.95	No	Select	$-	$0.25	$0.25	$0.25	$0.75
7/26/21	Monday	0			100%	Yes	3	1.11	Yes	3	1.11	Yes	2	0.95	No	Select	$-	$0.25	$0.25	$0.25	$0.75
7/27/21	Tuesday	0	N/A		100%	Yes	3	1.11	Yes	3	1.11	Yes	3	1.11	No	Select	$-	$0.25	$0.25	$0.25	$0.75
7/28/21	Wednesday	0			100%	No			Yes	2	0.95	Yes	2	0.95	No	Select	$-	$-	$0.25	$0.25	$0.50

Date	Day	#Cigarettes	Environment	Social	TI	CO Level 1	%COHb	CO Level 2	%COHB	CO Level 3	%COHB	Cotinine	Above/Below	Vouchers	Total
7/29/21	Thursday	0			100%	Yes 3	1.11	Yes 3	1.11	Yes 3	1.11	Yes	Below	$10.00 $0.25 $0.25 $0.25	$1.75
7/30/21	Friday	0			100%	Yes 2	0.95	Yes 3	1.11	No		No	Select	$-0.25 $0.25 $0.25 $-0.25	$0.50
7/31/21	Saturday	22			100%	Yes 2	0.95	Yes 8	1.91	Yes 17	3.35	No	Select	$-0.25 $0.25 $0.25 $0.25	$0.75
8/1/21	Sunday	0			100%	Yes 7	1.75	Yes 3	1.11	Yes 2	0.95	No	Below	$-0.25 $0.25 $0.25 $0.25	$1.75
Total Phase															**$12.00**
8/2/21	Monday	0	Yes	Yes	100%	Yes 2	0.95	Yes 2	0.95	Yes 1	0.79	Yes	Above	$10.00 $0.25 $0.25 $0.25	$1.75

Condition/Function Based

Date	Day	#Cigarettes	Environment	Social	TI1	CLOe1	v el	%COHb	CLOe2	v el	%COHB	CLOe3	v el	%COHB	Cotinine	Above/Below	Vhoeurcs				Total
8/3/21	Tuesday	0	Yes	Yes	100%	Yes	2	0.95	Yes	2	0.95	Yes	2	0.95	No	Select	$-.25	$0.25	$0.25	$0.25	$0.75
8/4/21	Wednesday	0	Yes	Yes	100%	Yes	2	0.95	Yes	1	0.79	No			No	Select	$-.25	$0.25	$0-	$-	$0.50
8/5/21	Thursday	0	Yes	Yes	100%	Yes	2	0.95	Yes	2	0.95	No			Yes	Below	$1.00	$0.25	$0.25	$-	$1.50
8/6/21	Friday	12	Yes	Yes	100%	Yes	2	0.95	Yes	2	0.95	Yes	2	0.95	No	Select	$-.25	$0.25	$0.25	$0.25	$0.75
8/7/21	Saturday	0	Yes	Yes	100%	Yes	8	1.91	Yes	5	1.43	Yes	3	1.11	No	Select	$-.25	$0.25	$0.25	$0.25	$0.75
8/8/21	Sunday	0	Yes	Yes	100%	Yes	2	0.95	Yes	3	1.11	No			No	Select	$-.25	$0.25	$0-	$-	$0.50

8/9/21	Monday	0	Yes	Yes	100%	Yes	2	0.95	Yes	2	0.95	Yes	2	0.95	No	Select	$-	$0.25	$0.25	$0.25	$0.75
8/10/21	Tuesday	0	Yes	Yes	100%	Yes	2	0.95	Yes	3	1.11	Yes	3	1.11	Yes	Below	$1.00	$0.25	$0.25	$0.25	$1.75
8/11/21	Wednesday	0	Yes	Yes	100%	Yes	3	1.11	Yes	3	1.11	Yes	3	1.11	No	Select	$-	$0.25	$0.25	$0.25	$0.75
8/12/21	Thursday	0	Yes	Yes	100%	Yes	3	1.11	Yes	3	1.11	Yes	2	0.95	No	Select	$-	$0.25	$0.25	$0.25	$0.75
8/13/21	Friday	19	Yes	Yes	100%	No			Yes	3	1.11	Yes	2	0.95	No	Select	$-	$-	$0.25	$0.25	$0.50
8/14/21	Saturday	3	Yes	Yes	100%	Yes	4	1.27	No			Yes	5	1.43	No	Select	$-	$0.25	$-	$0.25	$0.50
8/15/21	Sunday	0	Yes	Yes	100%	No			Yes	3	1.11	Yes	2	0.95	Yes	Above	$1.00	$-	$0.25	$0.25	$1.50

Date	Day	#Cigarettes	Environment	Social	TI1	CL Oe 1 vel	%COHb	CL Oe 2 vel	%COHB	CL Oe 3 vel	%COHB	Cotinine	Above/Below	Vhoeurcs				Total
8/16/21	Monday	0	Yes	Yes	100%	Yes	2	0.95	No		Yes	2	0.95	No	Select	$-.25	$0.25	$-.25	$0.00	$0.50
8/17/21	Tuesday	0	Yes	Yes	100%	Yes	2	0.95	No		Yes	2	0.95	No	Select	$-.25	$0.25	$-.25	$0.00	$0.50
8/18/21	Wednesday	0	Yes	Yes	100%	Yes	2	0.95	Yes	2	0.95	Yes	2	0.95	No	Select	$-.25	$0.25	$0.25	$0.25	$0.75
8/19/21	Thursday	0	Yes	Yes	100%	No			Yes	2	0.95	Yes	2	0.95	No	Select	$-.-	$-.25	$0.25	$0.00	$0.50
8/20/21	Friday	19	Yes	Yes	100%	Yes	2	0.95	No		Yes	2	0.95	No	Select	$-.25	$0.25	$-.25	$0.00	$0.50
8/21/21	Saturday	13	Yes	Yes	100%	No			No		No				No	Select	$-	$-	$-	$-	$-
8/22	Sunday	0	Yes	Yes	100%	No			No		No				No	Select	$-	$-	$-	$-	$-

Date	Day	#Cigarettes	Environment	Social	TI	CLOe1 vel	%COHb	CLOe2 vel	%COHB	CLOe3 vel	%COHB	Cotinine	Above/Below	Vhoeurcs				Total
/21					100%													
8/23/21	Monday	0	Yes	Yes	100%	No		No		Yes 2	0.95	Yes	Above	$1.00	$-	$-	$0.25	$1.25
8/24/21	Tuesday	0	Yes	Yes	100%	Yes 2	0.95	Yes 2	0.95	Yes 3	1.11	No	Select	$-	$0.25	$0.25	$0.25	$0.75
8/25/21	Wednesday	0	Yes	Yes	100%	Yes 3	1.11	Yes 2	0.95	No		No	Select	$-	$0.25	$0.25	$-	$0.50
8/26/21	Thursday	0	Yes	Yes	100%	Yes 3	1.11	No		No		No	Select	$-	$0.25	$-	$-	$0.25
8/27/21	Friday	0	Yes	Yes	100%	Yes 1	0.79	Yes 2	0.95	Yes 2	0.95	Yes	Below	$1.00	$0.25	$0.25	$0.25	$1.75
8/28/21	Saturday	13	Yes	Yes	100%	Yes 2	0.95	Yes 2	0.95	Yes 9	2.07	No	Select	$-	$0.	$0.	$0.	$0.

		Participant Entered			Researcher Entered																
Date	Day	#Cigarettes	Environment	Social	TI	CLOe1	vel	%COHb	CLOe2	vel	%COHB	CLOe3	vel	%COHB	Cotinine	Above/Below	Vhoeurs				Total
																		$.25	$.25	$.75	
8/29/21	Sunday	0	Yes	Yes	100%	Yes	3	1.11	Yes	3	1.11	Yes	2	0.95	No	Select	$-	$0.25	$0.25	$0.25	$0.75
Total Phase																					**$21.75**
8/30/21	Monday	0			100%	Yes	2	0.95	No			Yes	2	0.95	Yes	Above	$1.00	$0.25	$-	$0.25	$1.50
8/31/21	Tuesday	0	N/A		100%	Yes	1	0.79	No			Yes	1	0.79	No	Select	$-	$0.25	$-	$0.25	$0.50
9/1/21	Wednesday	0			100%	Yes	2	0.95	Yes	2	0.95	Yes	3	1.11	No	Select	$-	$0.25	$0.25	$0.25	$0.75

Date	Day	#Cigarettes	Environment	Social	TI 1	CO Level 1	%COHb	CO Level 2	%COHB	CO Level 3	%COHB	Cotinine	Above/Below	Vouchers				Total
9/2/21	Thursday	0			100%	Yes 2	0.95	No		Yes 1	0.79	Yes	Below	$1.00	$0.25	$-	$0.25	$1.50
9/3/21	Friday	0			100%	Yes 1	0.79	No		No		No	Select	$-	$0.25	$-	$-	$0.25
9/4/21	Saturday	13			100%	No		Yes 2	0.95	No		No	Select	$-	$-	$0.25	$-	$0.25
9/5/21	Sunday	3			100%	Yes 5	1.43	Yes 4	1.27	Yes 4	1.27	No	Select	$-	$0.25	$0.25	$0.25	$0.75
9/6/21	Monday	0	N/A		100%	Yes 2	0.95	Yes 2	0.95	Yes 2	0.95	No	Select	$-	$0.25	$0.25	$0.25	$0.75
9/7/21	Tuesday	0	N/A		100%	Yes 2	0.95	Yes 2	0.95	Yes 1	0.79	Yes	Below	$1.00	$0.25	$0.25	$0.25	$1.75

Condition: Baseline

Date	Day	#Cigar	Environ	So	TI1	CLOe1		%CO	CLOe2		%CO2	CLOe3		%CO3	Cotinine	Above/	Vhoe				Tot
9/8/21	Wednesday	0			100%	Yes	3	1.11	Yes	2	0.95	No			No	Select	$-	$0.25	$0.25	$-	$0.50
9/9/21	Thursday	0			100%	Yes	2	0.95	Yes	2	0.95	Yes	2	0.95	No	Select	$-	$0.25	$0.25	$0.25	$0.75
9/10/21	Friday	3			100%	Yes	2	0.95	No			Yes	2	0.95	Yes	Below	$1.00	$0.25	$-	$0.25	$1.50
9/11/21	Saturday	4			100%	Yes	3	1.11	Yes	3	1.11	Yes	8	1.91	No	Select	$-	$0.25	$0.25	$0.25	$0.75
9/12/21	Sunday	3			100%	Yes	3	1.11	Yes	3	1.11	Yes	7	1.75	No	Select	$-	$0.25	$0.25	$0.25	$0.75
Total Phase																				**$12.25**

Participant Entered | Researcher Entered

Condition: Voucher Based

		ettes	ment	cial		vel	Hb	vel	HB	vel	HB		Below	urcs				al
9/13/21	Monday	0			100%	Yes	4	1.27	Yes	2	0.95	Yes	2	0.95	No	Select	$-	$0.25	$0.30	$0.35	$0.90
9/14/21	Tuesday	0			100%	Yes	2	0.95	Yes	2	0.95	Yes	2	0.95	Yes	Below	$1.00	$0.40	$0.45	$0.55	$2.35
9/15/21	Wednesday	0			100%	Yes	2	0.95	Yes	2	0.95	Yes	2	0.10	No	Select	$-	$0.55	$0.60	$0.65	$1.80
9/16/21	Thursday	0	N/A		100%	Yes	2	0.95	Yes	2	0.95	Yes	1	0.79	No	Select	$-	$0.70	$0.75	$0.80	$2.25
9/17/21	Friday	3			100%	Yes	2	0.95	Yes	2	0.95	No				Yes	Below	$1.00	$0.80	$0.90	$-	$2.75
9/18/21	Saturday	9			100%	No			No			No			No	Select	$-	$-	$-	$-	$-
9/19/21	Sunday	0			100%	No			No			No			No	Select	$-	$-	$-	$-	$-

Condition: Voucher Based

Date	Day	#Cigarettes	Environment	Social	TI	CO1	%COHb	CO2	%COHB	CO3	%COHB	Cotinine	Above/Below	Vouchers				Total
9/20/21	Monday	0	N/A		100%	Yes 2	0.95	Yes 3	1.11	Yes 2	0.95	No	Select	$-	$0.25	$0.25	$0.95	$1.45
9/21/21	Tuesday	0			100%	Yes 1	0.79	Yes 2	0.95	No		No	Select	$-	$1.00	$1.05	$-	$2.05
9/22/21	Wednesday	0			100%	Yes 2	0.95	Yes 2	0.95	Yes 1	0.79	No	Select	$-	$0.25	$0.25	$1.10	$1.60
9/23/21	Thursday	0			100%	No		Yes 2	0.95	Yes 3	1.11	No	Select	$-	$-	$0.25	$0.25	$0.50
9/24/21	Friday	0			100%	Yes 2	0.95	Yes 2	0.95	Yes 2	0.95	Yes	Below	$1.00	$1.15	$1.20	$1.25	$4.60
9/25/21	Saturday	2			100%	Yes 2	0.95	Yes 2	0.95	No		No	Select	$-	$1.30	$1.35	$-	$2.65

Date	Day	#Cigarettes	Environment	Social	TI	CL Oe1 vel	%COHb	CL Oe2 vel	%COHB	CL Oe3 vel	%COHB	Continue	Above/Below	Vhoeurcs				Total
9/26/21	Sunday	0			100%	Yes 3	1.11	Yes 3	1.11	Yes 2	0.95	No	Select	$ -	$0.25	$0.25	$1.40	$1.90
9/27/21	Monday	0			100%	Yes 2	0.95	Yes 2	0.95	Yes 1	0.79	No	Select	$ -	$1.45	$1.50	$1.55	$4.50
9/28/21	Tuesday	0			100%	Yes 2	0.95	Yes 2	0.95	No		No	Select	$ -	$1.60	$1.65	$ -	$3.25
9/29/21	Wednesday	0	N/A		100%	Yes 2	0.95	Yes 2	0.95	Yes 2	0.95	No	Select	$ -	$0.25	$0.25	$1.70	$2.20
9/30/21	Thursday	0			100%	Yes 2	0.95	Yes 2	0.95	Yes 2	0.95	No	Select	$ -	$1.75	$1.80	$1.85	$5.40
10/1/21	Friday	3			100%	Yes 1	0.79	Yes 2	0.95	No		No	Select	$ -	$1.90	$1.95	$ -	$3.85

Conditions/Voucher Based

Date	Day	#Cigarettes	Environment	Social	TI1	CLOe1	vel	%COHb	CLOe2	vel	%COHB	CLOe3	vel	%COHB	Cotinine	Above/Below		Vhoeurcs			Total
10/2/21	Saturday	0			100%	No			Yes	4	1.27	No			No	Select	$-	$-	$0.25	$-	$0.25
10/3/21	Sunday	0			100%	Yes	2	0.95	Yes	2	0.95	Yes	2	0.95	No	Select	$-.25	$0.25	$0.25	$2.00	$2.50
10/4/21	Monday	0	N/A		100%	Yes	2	0.95	Yes	2	0.95	Yes	2	0.95	No	Select	$-	$2.05	$2.10	$2.15	$6.30
10/5/21	Tuesday	0			100%	No			Yes	2	0.95	Yes	2	0.95	No	Select	$-	$-	$0.25	$0.25	$0.50
10/6/21	Wednesday	0			100%	Yes	2	0.95	Yes	2	0.95	No			No	Select	$-	$2.20	$2.25	$-	$4.45
10/7/21	Thursday	0			100%	Yes	2	0.95	Yes	2	0.95	Yes	2	0.95	Yes	Below	$1.00	$0.25	$0.25	$2.30	$3.80

10/8/21	Friday	4	100%	Yes	2	0.95	Yes	2	0.95	No		No	Select	$-	$2.35	$2.40	$-	$4.75
10/9/21	Saturday	11	100%	No			No			No		No	Select	$-	$-	$-	$-	$-
10/10/21	Sunday	0	100%	No			No			No		No	Select	$-	$-	$-	$-	$-
Total Phase																		$66.55

Note. This table illustrates participant 2's study raw data & voucher earnings.

Table 9

Participant 2: Maintenance Probe/Social Validity Questionnaire

At this time, are you currently ?

-Yes, significantly less than before the study

If no: What have you found to be contributing to your success?

If yes: What have you found to be contributing factors in starting or continuing to smoke?

It's a habit, not a physical thing, not a mental thing, associated with drinking

Do you find the current study to be useful (Function based cessation), if so, why, and if not, why not?

-I do, I think about each cigarette, and the scoring on the monitor, you want to be better than the last time, the reminders

helped, and having to count the number of cigarettes What did
you enjoy about this study?
**-The equipment was cool and the charting and graphing was
cool, and was so easy** What did you not enjoy about this study?
**-Felt guilty when I forgot, but I really liked the study, because
researcher isn't a stranger** What changes would you suggest for
research in the future?
**-The questions didn't really relate to casual smokers
(what circumstances)** Did you feel that you played an
active role in selecting your own intervention?
**-I honestly did, I played the primary role based on wanting to be
successful**

Note: This table illustrates a Maintenance Probe/Social Validity

Questionnaire used to follow up on Participant 2's behavior

following the conclusion of the experiment.

Participant 3

Participant 3 was a 45-year-old White male whom reported

working full-time and had completed a Bachelor's degree. He

reported that COVID had increased his behavior. There was no

concern in financial uncertainty affecting his ability to access

cigarettes through the duration of the study. He reported that the

primary function of was that he was addicted to cigarettes and his

reason for wanting to quit is for health reasons (Table 10).

Table 10

*Participant 3: Pre-Assessment Self-Report Questionnaire &
Demographics*

1) Name: XXX

2) Age: 45

3) Gender: Male

4) Race/ethnicity: White

5) Highest level of education you've completed: Bachelors

6) Employment status: Full time   7) Contact Email: XXX 8) Address:

XXX

XXX

XXX

COVID-19 Impact

9) How has your behavior been affected by COVID-19?

Gone up

10) Has your frequency of changed given social distancing?

Yes

11) Has an income change prompted you to quit ? No

12) Will financial uncertainty as a result of COVID-19 affect your access to cigarettes? No

13) Will financial uncertainty as a result of COVID-19 affect your access to internet? No

Rationale

14) Why do you think you continue to smoke?

Addicted to cigarettes

15) What prompts you to want to quit now?

Health reasons

Note. This table displays Participant 3's Pre-Assessment Self-Report Questionnaire &

Demographics.

Participant 3's assessment results are displayed in Figure #7.

Participant 3's assessment result in the Attention function are as

follows: Friends/Family (+4 Agree, -3 Disagree), Other's Request

(+10 Agree, -0 Disagree), With Others (+6 Agree, -1 Disagree), Draw

Attention, (+0

Agree, -11 Disagree), New People (+3 Agree, -2 Disagree), Non-Approval (+0 Agree, -12

Disagree). Participant 3's assessment results in the Escape function are as follows: Break from

Tasks (+11 Agree, -0 Disagree), Remove Situation (+6 Agree, -0 Disagree), Remove People (+7

Agree, -0 Disagree), Remove Boredom, (+9 Agree, -1 Disagree), Remove Transit (+8 Agree, -1

Disagree), Avoid Task (+10 Agree, -0 Disagree). Participant 3's assessment results in the

Automatic Positive function are as follows: Buzz/Jump Start (+3 Agree, -4 Disagree), Smoke/Embers (+0 Agree, -12 Disagree), Cigarette Burn (+0 Agree, -11 Disagree), Cigarette

Smell, (+0 Agree, -5 Disagree), Flicking/Ashing (+3 Agree, -5 Disagree), Cigarette Taste (+3

Agree, -2 Disagree). Participant 3's assessment results in the

Automatic Negative function are as follows: Reduce Stress (+12

Agree, -0 Disagree), Reduce Appetite (+2 Agree, -5 Disagree),

Reduce Withdrawal (+7 Agree, -1 Disagree), Remove Pain, (+0

Agree, -12 Disagree), Remove Thoughts (+9 Agree, -1 Disagree),

Avoid Withdrawal (+7 Agree, -2 Disagree).

Participant 3's cessation data are shown in Figure #11 & raw data (Table 11). No features of this graph are different from the graph for Participant 1. In initial baseline (2 weeks), Participant 3 consumed 299 cigarettes, submitted 42/42 CO tests (ranging between 15 and 59ppm), and 4/4 cotinine tests (4 at criterion of a smoker and 0 at the criterion of a nonsmoker).

In the function based, 25% reduction phase, (2 weeks), participant 3 consumed 216 cigarettes (28% reduction), submitted 38/42 CO tests (ranging between 10 and 47ppm), and 4/4 cotinine tests (4 at the criterion of a smoker and 0 at the criterion of a non-smoker).

In the function based, 50% reduction phase, (2 weeks), participant 3 consumed 171 cigarettes (43% reduction), submitted 38/42 CO tests (ranging between 7 and 38 ppm), and 4/4 cotinine tests (4 at the criterion of a smoker and 0 at the criterion of a non-smoker).

In the return to baseline, (2 weeks), participant 3 consumed 202 cigarettes (32% reduction), submitted 35/42 CO tests (ranging between 9 and 36ppm), and 4/4 cotinine tests (4 at the criterion of a smoker and 0 at the criterion of a non-smoker).

In the voucher based phase, (4 weeks), participant 3 consumed 309 cigarettes (48% reduction), submitted 64/84 CO tests (ranging between 2 and 21ppm), and 8/8 cotinine tests (8 at the criterion of a smoker and 0 at the criterion of a non-smoker).

In initial Baseline (2 weeks), the data were of a high level, decreasing trend, and moderate variability (18-30 cigarettes). When advancing to the function based, 25% reduction phase (2 weeks), data were of a moderate level, increasing trend, and moderate variability (12-22 cigarettes). In the function based, 50% reduction phase (2 weeks), data were of a moderate level, decreasing trend, and low variability (10-16 cigarettes). In the return to Baseline, (2 weeks), data were of a moderate level, increasing trend, and high variability (10-21 cigarettes). In the Voucher Based phase (4 weeks), the data were of a moderate level, decreasing trend and moderate variability (8-17 cigarettes).

Participant 3's earnings (Table 3) were as follows for CO tests and Cotinine Tests: Baseline ($10.50/$4.00), function based ($19.00/$8.00), Baseline 2 ($8.75/$4.00), Voucher based ($2.50/$8.00) follow up ($10), for a grand total of $74.75.

At one-month follow-up (Table 12), Participant 3 self-reported that they continued to smoke, but their rate of was more or less where it was when he finished the study. He reported that stress/anxiety continue to have a significant impact on his behavior. In terms of how useful this study was for him, he identified that this research makes you more aware of when you're . As for participant enjoyment of the study, Participant 3 identified that working with the primary researcher was enjoyable, and he had not previously tracked the number of cigarettes he consumed, but was very interested in seeing his graphs. The participant did report the commitment to the study and remembering to submit tests was difficult, however, this participant had the highest adherence levels of all participants when it came to data reporting. Additionally, Participant 3 reported they felt they played an active role in the selection of their own intervention, which may lend itself, from a social significance standpoint to the level of effectiveness of his treatment.

Table 11

Participant 3: Raw Data

			Participant Entered	Researcher Entered

Date	Day	#Cigarettes	Escape	AutoNeg.	TI1	CLOe1 vel	%COHb	CLOe2 vel	%COHB	CLOe3 vel	%COHB	Cotinine	Above/Below	Vouchers	Total
12/6/21	Monday	20			100%	Yes 17	3.35	Yes 23	4.31	Yes 26	4.79	No	Select	$-0.25 0.25 0.25	$0.75
12/7/21	Tuesday	21			100%	Yes 21	3.99	Yes 21	3.99	Yes 31	5.59	No	Select	$-0.25 0.25 0.25	$0.75
12/8/21	Wednesday	21			100%	Yes 22	4.15	Yes 27	4.95	Yes 32	5.75	Yes	Above	$1.00 0.25 0.25	$1.75
12/9/21	Thursday	19	N/A		100%	Yes 24	4.47	Yes 31	5.59	Yes 28	5.11	No	Select	$-0.25 0.25 0.25	$0.75
12/10/21	Friday	21			100%	Yes 21	3.99	Yes 31	5.59	Yes 42	7.35	No	Select	$-0.25 0.25 0.25	$0.75
12/11/21	Saturday	25			100%	Yes 21	3.99	Yes 52	8.95	Yes 47	8.15	Yes	Above	$1.00 0.25 0.25	$1.75
12/12/21	Sunday	30			100	Yes 22	4.15	Yes 59	10.07	Yes 49	8.47	No	Select	$-0.25	$0.

Date	Day	#Cigarettes	Escape	Auto Neg.	ATI / 0%	CO Level 1	%COHb	CO Level 2	%COHB	CO Level 3	%COHB	Cotinine	Above/Below	Vouchers				Total
					0%												$0.25	$0.25 / $0.75
12/13/21	Monday	18			100%	Yes 15	3.03	Yes 34	6.07	Yes 44	7.67	No	Select	$-.25	0.25	0.25	0.25	$0.75
12/14/21	Tuesday	18			100%	Yes 22	4.15	Yes 36	6.39	Yes 40	7.03	Yes	Above	$1.00	0.25	0.25	0.25	$1.75
12/15/21	Wednesday	18	N/A		100%	Yes 29	5.27	Yes 32	5.75	Yes 42	7.35	No	Select	$-.25	0.25	0.25	0.25	$0.75
12/16/21	Thursday	20		A	100%	Yes 32	5.75	Yes 45	7.83	Yes 50	8.63	No	Select	$-.25	0.25	0.25	0.25	$0.75
12/17/21	Friday	23			100%	Yes 17	3.35	Yes 39	6.87	Yes 41	7.19	Yes	Above	$1.00	0.25	0.25	0.25	$1.75
12/18/21	Saturday	25			100%	Yes 35	6.23	Yes 51	8.79	Yes 54	9.27	No	Select	$-.25	0.25	0.25	0.25	$0.75

175

Date	Day	#Cigarettes	Escapet	AutoNeg.	TI	CLOe1 vel	%COHb	CLOe2 vel	%COHB	CLOe3 vel	%COHB	Cotinine	Above/Below	Vhoeursc	Total
12/19/21	Sunday	21			100%	Yes 16	3.19	Yes 28	5.11	Yes 47	8.15	No	Select	$-.25 0.2255	$0.775
Total Phase															**$14.50**
12/20/21	Monday	15	Yes	Yes	1.00	Yes 22	4.15	Yes 32	5.75	Yes 34	6.07	No	Select	$-.25 0.2255	$0.775
12/21/21	Tuesday	16	Yes	Yes	1.00	Yes 23	4.31	Yes 28	5.11	Yes 36	6.39	Yes	Above	$1.00 2.2255	$1.75
12/22/21	Wednesday	15	Yes	Yes	1.00	Yes 24	4.47	Yes 30	5.43	Yes 31	5.59	No	Select	$-.25 0.2255	$0.775
12/23/21	Thursday	16	Yes	Yes	1.00	Yes 24	4.47	Yes 29	5.27	Yes 38	6.71	No	Select	$-.25 0.2255	$0.775

Condition: FunctionBased

12/24/21	Friday	14	Yes	Yes	1.00	Yes	18	3.51	Yes	22	4.15	Yes	25	4.63	No	Select	$-	0.25	0.25	0.25	**$0.75**
12/25/21	Saturday	12	Yes	Yes	1.00	No			Yes	19	3.67	Yes	25	4.63	Yes	Above	$1.00	$-	0.25	0.25	**$1.50**
12/26/21	Sunday	14	Yes	Yes	1.00	Yes	16	3.19	Yes	19	3.67	Yes	35	6.23	No	Select	$-	0.25	0.25	0.25	**$0.75**
Date	**Day**	**#Cigarettes**	**Escape**	**Auto Neg.**	**TI**	**CO1**	**Level**	**%COHb**	**CO2**	**Level**	**%COHB**	**CO3**	**Level**	**%COHB**	**Cotinine**	**Above/Below**	**Vouchers**				**Total**
12/27/21	Monday	18	Yes	Yes	1.00	Yes	31	5.59	Yes	37	6.55	Yes	36	6.39	No	Select	$-	0.25	0.25	0.25	**$0.75**
12/28/21	Tuesday	20	Yes	Yes	1.00	Yes	22	4.15	Yes	38	6.71	Yes	47	8.15	Yes	Above	$1.00	0.25	0.25	0.25	**$1.75**
12/29/21	Wednesday	18	Yes	Yes	1.00	No			Yes	36	6.39	Yes	35	6.23	No	Select	$-	$-	0.25	0.25	**$0.50**
12/30/21	Thursday	18	Yes	Yes	1.00	No			Yes	32	5.75	Yes	42	7.35	No	Select	$-	$-	0.		**$0.**

Date	Day	#Cigarettes	Escaupet	Aut o Neg.	TI	CLOe 1 vel	%COHb	CLOe 2 vel	%COHB	CLOe 3 vel	%COHB	Cotinine	Above/Below	Vhoeursc	Total
														25 25	25
12/31/21	Friday	22	Yes	Yes	1.00	Yes 42	7.35	Yes 38	6.71	Yes 33	5.91	Yes	Above	$1.00 0.25 0.25 0.25	$1.75
1/1/22	Saturday	15	Yes	Yes	1.00	Yes 30	5.43	No		Yes 32	5.75	No	Select	$- 0.25 $- 0.25	$0.50
1/2/22	Sunday	13	Yes	Yes	1.00	Yes 10	2.23	Yes 23	4.31	Yes 33	5.91	No	Select	$- 0.25 0.25 0.25	$0.75
Total Phase															**$13.25**
Date	**Day**	**#Cigarettes**	**Escaupet**	**Aut o Neg.**	**TI**	**CLOe 1 vel**	**%COHb**	**CLOe 2 vel**	**%COHB**	**CLOe 3 vel**	**%COHB**	**Cotinine**	**Above/Below**	**Vhoeursc**	**Total**
1/3/22	Monday	16	Yes	Yes	1.00	No		Yes 36	6.39	Yes 38	6.71	No	Select	$- $- 0.25 0.25	$0.50
1/4/22	Tuesday	14	Yes	Yes	1.00	Yes 19	3.67	Yes 28	5.11	Yes 30	5.43	No	Select	$- 0.25	$0.

Date	Day	#Cigarettes	Escape	Auto Neg.	TI	CLOe1	%COHb	CLOe2	%COHB	CLOe3	%COHB	Cotinine	Above/Below	Vhoeurs c	Total
														0.25 0.25 0.75	$7.75
1/5/22	Wednesday	14	Yes	Yes	1.00	Yes 10	2.23	Yes 29	5.27	Yes 23	4.31	Yes	Above	$1.00 0.25 0.25 0.25	$1.75
1/6/22	Thursday	13	Yes	Yes	1.00	Yes 14	2.87	Yes 24	4.47	Yes 26	4.79	No	Select	$- 0.25 0.25 0.25	$0.75
1/7/22	Friday	11	Yes	Yes	1.00	Yes 12	2.55	Yes 29	5.27	Yes 25	4.63	No	Select	$- 0.25 0.25 0.25	$0.75
1/8/22	Saturday	12	Yes	Yes	1.00	Yes 10	2.23	Yes 24	4.47	Yes 29	5.27	Yes	Above	$1.00 0.25 0.25 0.25	$1.75
1/9/22	Sunday	11	Yes	Yes	1.00	Yes 16	3.19	Yes 19	3.67	Yes 30	5.43	No	Select	$- 0.25 0.25 0.25	$0.75
Date	Day	#Cigarettes	Escape	Auto Neg.	TI	CLOe1	%COHb	CLOe2	%COHB	CLOe3	%COHB	Cotinine	Above/Below	Vhoeurs c	Total
1/10/22	Monday	11	Yes	Yes	1.00	No		Yes 19	3.67	Yes 20	3.83	No	Select	$- $- 0.25 0.25	$0.50

Date	Day																				
1/11/22	Tuesday	10	Yes	Yes	1.00	No			Yes	18	3.51	Yes	21	3.99	No	Select	$-	$-	0.25	0.25	$0.50
1/12/22	Wednesday	11	Yes	Yes	1.00	Yes	11	2.39	Yes	23	4.31	Yes	23	4.31	Yes	Above	$1.00	0.25	0.25	0.25	$1.75
1/13/22	Thursday	10	Yes	Yes	1.00	No			Yes	15	3.03	Yes	22	4.15	No	Select	$-	$-	0.25	$0.25	$0.50
1/14/22	Friday	13	Yes	Yes	1.00	Yes	12	2.55	Yes	17	3.35	Yes	21	3.99	No	Select	$-	0.25	0.25	0.25	$0.75
1/15/22	Saturday	13	Yes	Yes	1.00	Yes	10	2.23	Yes	15	3.03	Yes	18	3.51	Yes	Above	$1.00	0.25	0.25	0.25	$1.75
1/16/22	Sunday	12	Yes	Yes	1.00	Yes	7	1.75	Yes	13	2.71	Yes	15	3.03	No	Select	$-	0.25	0.25	0.25	$0.75
Total Phase																					$13.50

	Particie pantd Enter				Research er Entered												
Date	Day	#Cigarettes	Escape	Auto Neg.	TI	CLOe1	%COHb	CLOe2	%COHB	CLOe3	%COHB	Cotinine	Above/Below	Vhoeursc				Total
1/17/22	Monday	13		N/A	1.00	No		Yes 22	4.15	Yes 14	2.87	No	Select	$-	$-	0.25	0.25	$0.50
1/18/22	Tuesday	10			100%	No		Yes 10	2.23	Yes 20	3.83	No	Select	$-	$-	0.25	0.25	$0.50
1/19/22	Wednesday	13			100%	Yes 19	3.67	Yes 22	4.15	Yes 15	2.03	Yes	Above	$1.00	0.25	0.25	0.25	$1.75
1/20/22	Thursday	12			100%	No		Yes 17	3.35	Yes 16	3.19	No	Select	$-	$-	0.25	0.25	$0.50
1/21/22	Friday	14			100%	No		No		Yes 15	3.03	No	Select	$-	$-	$-	0.25	$0.25
1/22/22	Saturday	16			100%	No		Yes 29	5.27	Yes 16	3.19	Yes	Above	$1.00	$-	0.25	0.25	$1.50

Date	Day	#Cigarettes	Escaupe	Auto Neg.	ATI	CLOe1 Level	%COHb	CLOe2 Level	%CO HB	CLOe3 Level	%CO HB	Cotinine	Above/Below	Vhoeursc	Total
1/23/22	Sunday	11			100%	Yes 9		Yes 9		Yes 11	2.39	No	Select	$- / 0.25 / 0.25 / 0.25	$0.75
1/24/22	Monday	17			100%	No		Yes 24	4.47	Yes 31	5.59	No	Select	$- / $- / 0.25 / 0.25	$0.50
1/25/22	Tuesday	14			100%	Yes 17	3.35	Yes 22	4.15	Yes 15	3.03	No	Select	$- / 0.25 / 0.25 / 0.25	$0.75
1/26/22	Wednesday	15	N/A		100%	Yes 11	2.39	Yes 12	2.55	Yes 25	4.63	Yes	Above	$1.00 / 0.25 / 0.25 / 0.25	$1.75
1/27/22	Thursday	15			100%	Yes 13	2.71	Yes 16	3.19	Yes 19	3.67	No	Select	$- / 0.25 / 0.25 / 0.25	$0.75
1/28/22	Friday	14			100%	Yes 18	3.51	Yes 20	3.83	Yes 11	2.39	No	Select	$- / 0.25 / 0.25 / 0.25	$0.75
1/29/22	Saturday	18			100%	Yes 25	4.63	Yes 27	4.95	Yes 36	6.39	Yes	Above	$1.00 / 0.25 / 0.25 / 0.25	$1.75

Date	Day	#Cigarettes	Escape	Auto to Neg.	TI	CLO1	Level	%COOHb	CLO2	Level	%COOHB	CLO3	Level	%COOHB	Continue	Above/Below	Vouchers	Total
																		$0.00
1/30/22	Sunday	21			100%	Yes	23	4.31	Yes	26	4.79	Yes	36	6.39	No	Select	$- $0.25 $0.25 $0.25	$0.75
Total Phase																		**$12.75**

		Participant Entered			Researcher Entered													
Date	Day	#Cigarettes	Escape	Auto to Neg.	TI	CLO1	Level	%COOHb	CLO2	Level	%COOHB	CLO3	Level	%COOHB	Continue	Above/Below	Vouchers	Total
1/31/22	Monday	14			100%	Yes	24	4.47	Yes	15	3.03	Yes	10	2.23	No	Select	$- $- $- $-	$-
2/1/22	Tuesday	13		N/A	100%	No			Yes	15	3.03	Yes	14	2.87	No	Select	$- $- $- $-	$-
2/2/22	Wednesday	12			100%	Yes	11	2.39	No			Yes	11	2.39	Yes	Above	$1.00 $- $- $-	$1.00

183

Date	Day	#Cigarettes	Escapet	AutoNeg.	TI	CLOe1	Level	%COOHb	CLOe2	Level	%COOHB	CLOe3	Level	%COOHB	Cotinine	Above/Below	Vouchers				Total
2/3/22	Thursday	12			100%	Yes	4	1.27	Yes	7	1.75	Yes	16	3.19	No	Select	$-	$0.25	$-	$-	$0.25
2/4/22	Friday	13			100%	Yes	4	1.27	Yes	14	2.87	Yes	18	3.51	No	Select	$-	$0.25	$-	$-	$0.25
2/5/22	Saturday	10			100%	Yes	4	1.27	Yes	11	2.39	Yes	11	2.39	Yes	Above	$1.00	$0.25	$-	$-	$1.25
2/6/22	Sunday	13			100%	Yes	8	1.91	Yes	19	3.67	Yes	10	2.23	No	Select	$-	$-	$-	$-	$-
Date	Day	#Cigarettes	Escapet	AutoNeg.	TI	CLOe1	Level	%COOHb	CLOe2	Level	%COOHB	CLOe3	Level	%COOHB	Cotinine	Above/Below	Vouchers				Total
2/7/22	Monday	12			100%	Yes	6	1.59	Yes	6	1.59	Yes	10	2.23	No	Select	$-	$-	$-	$-	$-
2/8/22	Tuesday	9		N/A	100%	Yes	4	1.27	No			Yes	8	1.91	No	Select	$-	$0.25	$-	$-	$0.25
2/9/22	Wednesday	11			100%	No			Yes	11	2.39	Yes	8	1.91	No	Select	$-	$-	$-	$-	$-

Date	Day	#Cigarettes	Escape	Auto Neg.	TI	CL Oe 1	% COOHb	CL Oe 2 vel	% COOHB	CL Oe 3 vel	% COHB	Cotinine	Above/Below	Vouchers				Total
2/10/22	Thursday	9			100%	Yes	5	1.43	Yes	6	1.59	Yes	11	2.39	Yes	Above	$1.00	$-	$-	$-	$1.00
2/11/22	Friday	10			100%	Yes	3	1.11	Yes	12	2.55	Yes	8	1.91	No	Select	$-	$0.25	$-	$-	$0.25
2/12/22	Saturday	15			100%	Yes	5	1.43	Yes	16	3.19	Yes	10	2.23	No	Select	$-	$-	$-	$-	$-
2/13/22	Sunday	17			100%	No			Yes	20	3.67	Yes	10	2.23	Yes	Above	$1.00	$-	$-	$-	$1.00

Date	Day	#Cigarettes	Escape	Auto Neg.	TI	CL Oe 1	% COOHb	CL Oe 2 vel	% COOHB	CL Oe 3 vel	% COHB	Cotinine	Above/Below	Vouchers				Total
2/14/22	Monday	13			100%	No			No			Yes	13	2.71	No	Select	$-	$-	$-	$-	$-
2/15/22	Tuesday	9	N/A		100%	No			No			Yes	9	1.59	No	Select	$-	$-	$-	$-	$-
2/16/22	Wednesday	11			100%	Yes	6	1.59	Yes	4	1.27	Yes	21	3.99	No	Select	$-	$-	$0.	$-	$0.

Conditions Voucher Based

Date	Day	#Cigarettes	Escape	Auto Neg.	TI1	CLOe vel	%COOeHb	CLOe2 vel	%COOeHB2	CLOe3 vel	%COOeHB3	Cotinine	Above/Below	Vouchers	Total
	sday				0%									25	**25**
2/17/22	Thursday	10			100%	No		No		Yes 7	1.75	Yes	Above	$1.00 $- $- $-	**$1.00**
2/18/22	Friday	9			100%	No		Yes 5	1.43	Yes 12	2.55	No	Select	$- $- $- $-	$-
2/19/22	Saturday	10			100%	Yes 4	1.27	No		Yes 11	2.39	No	Select	$- $0.25 $- $-	**$0.25**
2/20/22	Sunday	9			100%	Yes 4	1.27	Yes 11	2.39	Yes 6	1.59	Yes	Above	$1.00 $0.25 $- $-	**$1.25**
2/21/22	Monday	9	N/A		1.00	No		No		Yes 8	1.91	No	Select	$- $- $- $-	$-
2/22/22	Tuesday	9	N/A		1.00	No		Yes 15	3.03	Yes 8	1.91	No	Select	$- $- $- $-	$-
2/23/22	Wednesday	15	N/A		1.00	No		No		Yes 20	3.83	Yes	Above	$1.	**$1.**

Date	Day																		
	sday														00				00
2/24/22	Thursday	9	1.00	Yes	9	2.07	No			Yes	5	1.43	No	Select	$-	$-	$-	$-	$-
2/25/22	Friday	8	1.00	Yes	2	0.95	Yes	9	2.07	Yes	7	1.75	No	Select	$-	$0.25	$-	$-	$0.25
2/26/22	Saturday	10	1.00	Yes	4	1.27	Yes	6	1.59	Yes	8	1.91	Yes	Above	$1.00	$0.25	$-	$-	$1.25
2/27/22	Sunday	8	1.00	No			Yes	5	1.43	Yes	5	1.43	No	Select	$-	$-	$-	$-	$-
Total Phase																			$10.50

Note. This table illustrates participant 3's study raw data & voucher earnings.

Table 12

Participant 3: Maintenance Probe/Social Validity Questionnaire

At this time, are you currently ?
yes
If no: What have you found to be contributing to your success?
If yes: What have you found to be contributing factors in starting or continuing to smoke?

Stress/anxiety
Do you find the current study to be useful (Function based
cessation), if so, why, and if not, why not?
**I'll say yes, probably because it makes you more aware of
when you're , and accountability for how much you're** What
did you enjoy about this study?
**Besides getting to work with XXX, it was interesting to see how
much I smoked, and to get to see the graphs**
What did you not enjoy about this study?
The commitment, and remembering to do it
What changes would you suggest for research in the future?
I don't know what changes I could have made
Did you feel that you played an active role in selecting your
own intervention? **Yeah, I would say so**

Note: This table illustrates a Maintenance Probe/Social Validity

Questionnaire used to follow up on Participant 3's behavior

following the conclusion of the experiment.

Participant 4

Participant 4 was a 36-year-old Black nonbinary individual

who reported working fulltime and had completed some college.

They reported that COVID had increased their behavior. There was

no concern in financial uncertainty affecting their ability to access

cigarettes through the duration of the study. They reported that the

primary function of was trauma and "death related " where they

identified that 14 friends had passed away in the previous two years.

The primary reason for wanting to quit is that they never wanted to smoke, but it came with the nightlife job, and was connected to

COVID stress (Table 13).

Table 13

Participant 4: Pre-Assessment Self-Report Questionnaire & Demographics

1) Name: XXX
2) Age: 36
3) Gender: Nonbinary (They/Them)
4) Race/ethnicity: Black
5) Highest level of education you've completed: Some College
6) Employment status: Full Time   7) Contact Email: XXX 8) Address:

XXX

XXX

XXX

COVID-19 Impact

9) How has your behavior been affected by COVID-19?

Increased

10) Has your frequency of changed given social distancing?

Yes, Up

11) Has an income change prompted you to quit ? No

12) Will financial uncertainty as a result of COVID-19 affect your access to cigarettes? No

13) Will financial uncertainty as a result of COVID-19 affect your access to internet? No

Rationale

14) Why do you think you continue to smoke?

Death related (14 deaths in last 2 years),

Trauma 15) What prompts you to want to quit now?

Never really wanted to smoke, but came with nightlife job, connected to COVID stress

Note. This table displays Participant 4's Pre-Assessment Self-Report Questionnaire &

Demographics.

Participant 4's assessment results are displayed in Figure #8.

Participant 4's assessment result in the Attention function are as

follows: Friends/Family (+0 Agree, -6 Disagree), Other's

Request (+5 Agree, -1 Disagree), With Others (+0 Agree, -4 Disagree), Draw Attention, (+0

Agree, -9 Disagree), New People (+0 Agree, -5 Disagree), Non-Approval (+1 Agree, -6

Disagree). Participant 4's assessment results in the Escape function are as follows: Break from

Tasks (+1 Agree, -4 Disagree), Remove Situation (+1 Agree, -4 Disagree), Remove People (+2

Agree, -4 Disagree), Remove Boredom, (+1 Agree, -5 Disagree), Remove Transit (+0 Agree, -6

Disagree), Avoid Task (+1 Agree, -5 Disagree). Participant 4's assessment results in the

Automatic Positive function are as follows: Buzz/Jump Start (+2 Agree, -4 Disagree),

Smoke/Embers (+0 Agree, -6 Disagree), Cigarette Burn (+0 Agree, -9 Disagree), Cigarette

Smell, (+0 Agree, -7 Disagree), Flicking/Ashing (+0 Agree, -8 Disagree), Cigarette Taste (+0

Agree, -9 Disagree). Participant 4's assessment results in the Automatic Negative function are as follows: Reduce Stress (+7 Agree, -0 Disagree), Reduce Appetite (+0 Agree, -6 Disagree), Reduce Withdrawal (+1 Agree, -5 Disagree), Remove Pain, (+1 Agree, -5 Disagree), Remove Thoughts (+6 Agree, -0 Disagree), Avoid Withdrawal (+1 Agree, -5 Disagree).

Figure #12 shows Participant 4's cessation data & raw data (Table 14). No features of this graph are different from the graph for participant 1In initial baseline (2 weeks), Participant 4 consumed 20 cigarettes, submitted 42/42 CO tests (ranging between 1 and 7ppm), and 3/4 cotinine tests (2 at criterion of a smoker and 1 at the criterion of a non-smoker).

In the function based, 25% reduction phase, (1 week), Participant 4 consumed 2 cigarettes (80% reduction), submitted 15/21 CO tests (ranging between 1 and 4ppm), and 2/2 cotinine tests (1 at the criterion of a smoker and 1 at the criterion of a non-smoker).

At the end of week 3, Participant 4 no longer submitted the daily number of cigarettes, CO tests, or cotinine tests, and did not continue the study.

Participant 4's earnings (Table 3) were as follows for CO tests and Cotinine Tests:

Baseline ($9.75/$3.00) and function based ($3.75/$2.00), for a grand total of $18.50.

Participant 4 did not have a one-month follow-up as they did not complete the study. Given that this participant did not complete the study, they do not have maintenance and social validity results.

Table 14

Participant 4: Raw Data

			Participant Entered	Researcher Entered												
Condition:Baseline	Date	Day	#Cigarettes	AutoNeg.	TI1	CLO1 Level	%COHb	CLO2 Level	%COHb2	CLO3 Level	%COHB3	Cotinine	Above/Below	Vouchers			Total
	1/3/22	Monday	3		100%	Yes 6	1.59	Yes 8	1.91	Yes 6	1.59	Yes	Above	$1.00 $0.25 $0.25 $0.25			$1.75
	1/4/22	Tuesday	5	N/A	100%	Yes 2	0.95	Yes 4	1.27	Yes 7	1.75	No	Select	$-.25 $0.25 $0.25 $0.25			$0.75
	1/5/22	Wednesday	4		100%	Yes 4	1.27	Yes 4	1.27	Yes 4	0.95	No	Select	$-.25 $0.25 $0.25 $0.25			$0.75

Date	Day	#Cigarettes	Auto Neg.	TI	CO1	Level	%COHb	CO2	Level	%COHB	CO3	Level	%COHB	Cotinine	Above/Below	Vouchers				Total
1/6/22	Thursday	2		100%	Yes	7	1.75	Yes	7	1.75	Yes	4	1.27	Yes	Above	$1.00	$0.25	$0.25	$0.25	**$1.75**
1/7/22	Friday	2		100%	Yes	4	1.27	Yes	6	1.59	Yes	5	1.43	No	Select	$-.25	$0.25	$0.25	$0.25	**$0.75**
1/8/22	Saturday	0		100%	Yes	2	0.95	Yes	3	1.11	Yes	2	0.95	No	Select	$-.25	$0.25	$0.25	$0.25	**$0.75**
1/9/22	Sunday	0		100%	Yes	2	0.95	Yes	3	1.11	Yes	4	1.27	No	Select	$-.25	$0.25	$0.25	$0.25	**$0.75**
1/10/22	Monday	2	N / A	100%	No			No			No			No	Select	$-	$-	$-	$-	**$-**
1/11/22	Tuesday	0		100%	Yes	4	1.27	Yes	5	1.43	Yes	2	0.95	No	Select	$-.25	$0.25	$0.25	$0.25	**$0.75**

Date	Day	#Cigarettes	AutoN	TI	CLOe1	%COOHb	CLOe2 vel	%COOHB2	CLOe3 vel	%COOHB3	Cotinine	Above/Below	Vouchers				Total
1/12/22	Wednesday	0		100%	Yes 3	1.11	Yes 2	0.95	Yes 1	0.79	No	Select	$-	$0.25	$0.25	$0.25	$0.75
1/13/22	Thursday	0		100%	Yes 2	0.95	Yes 3	1.11	Yes 2	0.95	Yes	Below	$10.00	$0.25	$0.25	$0.25	$1.75
1/14/22	Friday	1		100%	Yes 5	1.43	Yes 3	1.11	Yes 2	0.95	No	Select	$-	$0.25	$0.25	$0.25	$0.75
1/15/22	Saturday	1		100%	Yes 2	0.95	Yes 3	1.11	Yes 3	1.11	No	Select	$-	$0.25	$0.25	$0.25	$0.75
1/16/22	Sunday	0		100%	Yes 3	1.11	Yes 3	1.11	Yes 3	1.11	No	Select	$-	$0.25	$0.25	$0.25	$0.75
Total Phase																	$12.75
Date	Day	#Cigarettes	AutoN	TI	CLOe1 vel	%COOHb	CLOe2 vel	%COOHB2	CLOe3 vel	%COOHB3	Cotinine	Above/Below	Vouchers				Total

					eg.															
1/17/21	Monday	0	Yes	100%	Yes	2	0.95	Yes	3	1.11	Yes	2	0.95	Yes	Below	$10.20	$0.25	$0.25	$0.25	$1.75
1/18/21	Tuesday	0	Yes	100%	Yes	1	0.79	Yes	2	0.95	Yes	2	0.95	No	Select	$-.25	$0.25	$0.25	$0.25	$0.75
1/19/21	Wednesday	0	Yes	100%	Yes	3	1.11	Yes	2	0.95	Yes	3	1.11	No	Select	$-.25	$0.25	$0.25	$0.25	$0.75
1/20/21	Thursday	1	Yes	100%	Yes	2	0.95	Yes	3	1.11	Yes	4	1.27	Yes	Above	$10.20	$0.25	$0.25	$0.25	$1.75
1/21/21	Friday	1	Yes	100%	Yes	3	1.11	Yes	3	1.11	Yes	2	0.95	No	Select	$-.25	$0.25	$0.25	$0.25	$0.75
1/22/21	Saturday		Select	0%	-			-			-			Select	Select					$-
1/23/21	Sunday		Select	0%	-			-			-			Select	Select					$-

Total Phase																								$5.75

Note. This table illustrates participant 4's study raw data & voucher earnings.

Chapter 7: Discussion

Participant 1

Participant 1's assessment results indicated primarily Escape and Automatic Negative functions. Remove Situation, Remove People, and Remove Transit were the primary maintaining variables surrounding the Escape function and Reduce Stress and Remove Thoughts from the Automatic Negative function. The behavior plan established for Participant 1 included separate components to address these function(s). For escape, the participant identified that cigarettes are a means by to escape/avoid aversive situations/people (social) and it is an activity that they do in transit. Additionally, Participant 1 identified that stress is a major factor in , which was correlated with the highest levels in the Automatic Negative function being Reduce Stress and

Remove Thoughts. The established behavior plan for the Escape function was as follows: "To escape an aversive social interaction that is terminated with a cigarette, reach out for quality social interaction from another individual, while in transit, select an incompatible behavior to do in the time you would otherwise be ." The established behavior plan for the Automatic Negative function was as follows:

"Increase exercise, and do replacement activities instead of a cigarette." For this participant, Remove Situation, Remove People, and Remove Transit are collateral to Reduce Stress & Remove Thoughts. Given that these sub-functions all fall within the greater negative reinforcement categories (Social Negative & Auto Negative), the participant created stress reduction strategies to address these functions. Lastly, the participant's intervention included a standardized planned titration (two weeks for 25% reduction, two weeks for 50% reduction, one week for 75% reduction, and one week for 100% reduction)as this research focus is cessation in the absence of nicotine replacement. In the initial demographic questionnaire, Participant 1's self-report (Table 3) also did identify Stress/Anxiety as a primary maintaining variable, but he did not specifically identify any of the Escape functions.

Participant 1's baseline was extended from the original two-week standardized plan to four weeks as the participant had left the country and did not have access to his carbon monoxide reader. After return, the carbon monoxide reader was rendered inoperable, and the primary researcher overnighted a new device to the participant (three days of data (CO Tests & Number of Cigarettes were not submitted as the study was placed on hold)). This phase change is labeled "Instrumentation Decay", however, the participant submitted a cotinine test during this span of time. In baseline, Participant 1's data were on a steady downtrend. Although many CO tests were missed, the cotinine tests confirm that this participant was still at the level of a smoker. When advancing to the 25% reduction function based phase, the participant was successful at meeting that criterion. For the 50% reduction and 75% reduction phases, the participant had demonstrated full cessation with the 100% reduction function based phase, and this is verified by the CO tests all reported under 4ppm and the cotinine tests at the level of a non-smoker. For the final week of the study (100% reduction + behavior plan), Participant 1 reported one cigarette, an instance of renewal, which the participant self-reported as a single drag, and the participant threw the cigarette out because it "tasted horrible". Additionally, on 9-9-2021, Participant 1 reported that a friend offered them a cigarette and he reported "telling myself not to buy." Given that this participant had demonstrated four weeks of full cessation at the phase threshold of 5% or 1 cigarette, the study was concluded and debriefing was provided. For this participant, the titration + function based behavior plan was successful in reducing his behavior from a baseline of 0-5 per day to 0 per day, a 100% reduction in . Additionally, this participant's CO tests and cotinine tests appear to be consistent with the self-report data on the number of cigarettes consumed, suggesting accuracy in reporting.

It is important to note that this suppression of responding across bassline and treatment may have been a product of tracking and self-reporting data (number of Cigarettes, CO, and Cotinine) as evidenced by a decreasing trend across baseline. By the same token, inconsistent submission of these tests would by nature decrease their effects on the suppression itself. In addition, if the tracking (in isolation) was the variable suppressing , the behavior would not have immediately dropped to 0 when advancing to the 50% reduction + behavior plan phase. would have slowly continued to suppress as it did between baseline and the function based 25% reduction phase f. In all, whether the effects of the cessation were a product of the tracking or the behavior plan augmented by the tracking (as a treatment package), the participant still reached the level of 100% reduction within the 10 week study. This result demonstrates the effectiveness of the participant's treatment plan, which was developed off the functional assessment.

Participant 2

Participant 2's assessment results almost exclusively indicated an Attention function. Friends/Family, Other's Request, With Others, and New People were indicated as the primary maintaining variables surrounding his . After further discussion with this participant, he indicated that he does not typically consume cigarettes during the week and smokes only while at the bar on weekends. As a consequence, the intervention established for Participant 2 included environmental arrangements and a self-management plan to address the Attention function(s). Given that the participant identified the individuals at the bar occasioning and the bar itself evoking behavior, the researcher and participant developed a behavior plan with plan oriented to alter current stimulus control involved in the participant's behavior. Participant 2 suggested to "Only bring a cigarette allowance to the bar/gathering", additionally, for the Attention function, Participant 2 suggested "having alcoholic beverages inside of an establishment where you cannot smoke, having the first alcoholic beverage without a cigarette, and limiting to (1) cigarette per alcoholic beverage, after the first." Lastly, the participant's intervention included a standardized planned titration plan as this research focused on cessation in the absence of nicotine replacement. Participant 2's self-report (Table 5) identified " as a habit" as the primary maintaining variable and did not specifically identify any Attention function(s).

Participant 2's baseline was the standard length (2 weeks) and there were two days where the individual self-reported , these data were a value of 2 and 22, the second being on a Saturday (the participant self-reported that all of these cigarettes were consumed at bar-time, before midnight). Given the length of baseline for a behavior that is intermittent but of an extremely high rate when it occurs, the highest data point was used as the baseline measure. When advancing to the 25% reduction function based phase, a similar pattern was seen relative to baseline, two high data points, both on Friday, and one data point with a value of 4 for Saturday, which the participant self-reported as a carryover from the previous evening (postmidnight). Even though the participant had two spikes in the data, he still met criterion to advance to the 50% reduction function based phase. Like with the 25% reduction phase, virtually the same pattern remained in the 50% reduction phase (only diverging by one cigarette). However, given the failure to meet the 50% reduction and to advance to the 75% reduction phase, the participant returned to baseline for two weeks. When returning to baseline, the behavior of maintained the same level as the previous phase on the following Saturday (potential carryover effect) with 3 additional cigarettes into the morning (post-bar). However, across the second weekend (Friday-Sunday), the total rate of was a total of 10 cigarettes (3, 4, 3), a significant decrease in rate relative to all other phases.

When advancing to the voucher based phase, the same pattern of cigarette consumption continued (Saturday, Saturday, Friday, Saturday), at the same time, the rates of had dropped dramatically relative to function based 25 and 50% reduction, (9, 3, 4, and 11).

The function based intervention was effective in reducing some of the variability regarding the daily number of cigarettes and may have been more successful in reducing rates had the condition been extended (e.g. additional time in the 50% reduction phase) since these data were in a downward trend in the 50% condition.

The voucher based phase reduced overall cigarette consumption to the lowest variability and lowest rates through the entire study. Additionally, Participant 2 contacted the progressive contingency most frequently with 61/84 opportunities (Table 12). Based on the data collected for this participant, across the first 8 weeks of the study there was virtually no- outside of the weekend (e.g., they would contact the voucher-based reinforcer every time, until the weekend.)

Regarding integrity of the CO tests, the cotinine results perfectly reflect the data that Participant 2 submitted. When the participant reported not-consuming cigarettes 2-3 days prior the cotinine test resulted in a pass, and when the participant reported that they had consumed cigarettes in that same amount of time the cotinine test reliably resulted in a fail. There was only one instance (first cotinine test) where the (2) cigarettes consumed the day prior resulted in a passed test. A consideration here is perhaps the cotinine test was not sensitive to this amount of cigarette consumption, the delay was too great (e.g., those cigarettes consumed in the morning of 7-20-2021 with the test in the evening of 7-21-2021), or the cotinine test was defective/utilized incorrectly. Outside of this instance, the cotinine tests were an overall excellent secondary measure to augment the self-report data. For this participant, the function based treatment package was effective at reducing from a baseline level of 22 cigarettes per week down to 13 cigarettes (41% reduction) in the 50% reduction + behavior plan phase. Additionally, the voucher based phase resulted in an average of 8 cigarettes (64% reduction) per week relative to baseline. At the same time, voucher based treatment methodologies (with progressive and resetting contingencies) are the most heavily researched cessation protocol, and in this case, produced an additional 23% reduction following a set titration + behavior plan. Given that the participant was allowed to select their own intervention in the voucher based phase it is unclear if the participant was continuing to utilize the behavior plan, if their behavior came under the stimulus control of the progressive-resetting contingency, or whether reduction was a product of both. In any case, a 41% reduction in , from a harm reduction (i.e., reducing the rate of a dangerous behavior, when abstinence is not probable/possible) standpoint is significant and demonstrates the potential effectiveness of the participant's treatment plan that was developed off the functional assessment. Secondly, a harm reduction approach is still a demonstration of behavior shifting in a socially significant direction- even if an individual never reaches full abstinence Lastly, this participant's CO tests and cotinine tests appear to be consistent with the self-report data on the number of cigarettes consumed, suggesting accuracy in reporting.

Participant 3

Participant 3's assessment results indicated significant multiple-control of Attention,

Escape, and Automatic Negative function(s). For the function of Attention, Other's Request and With Others were the highest. Every Escape function was at a level of +6 and above (Break from

Tasks, Remove Situation, Remove People, Remove Boredom, Remove Transit, and Avoid

Task). As for Automatic Negative function(s), Reduce Stress, Reduce

Withdrawal, Remove Thoughts, and Avoid Withdrawal were at the

highest levels. Given the strong levels of multiplecontrol, the

behavior plan established for Participant 3 included intervention

components that would address the highest levels of reported function

which was the best option for a selfmanagement plan that could be

accomplished with fidelity. When discussing these results with the

participant, he identified that the extreme majority of behavior

occurred in the absence of other individuals, which is why the

researcher and participant decided to not specifically target the

Attention function. However, treatment for the Attention function

would have involved competing/incompatible responses, which is a

component of the treatment for the Escape and Automatic Negative

function(s) already. In other words, we did not add a third treatment component specifically targeting Attention, as other function(s) treatment addresses this component already. To address the function of Escape, the participant's behavior plan was as follows: "Walking the dog in the absence of a cigarette embedded within planned breaks through the day." Secondly, to address the Automatic Negative function, the treatment plan was as follows: "Planned titration to address the Reduce/Avoid Withdrawal function and increase reading, listening to music, and playing games on the phone to addresses the Reduce Stress and Remove Thoughts components by creating a reinforcing, rich environment as an alternative to . To that effect, the intervention attempted to compete with the primary reinforcer (drug) by introducing a multitude of secondary reinforcer(s). Participant 3's self-report (Table 7) identified "addicted to cigarettes" as the primary maintaining variable and did not specifically identify any Attention, Escape, or stress related Automatic Negative function(s).

Participant 3's baseline was the standard length (2 weeks). This participant engaged in high levels of ranging from 18 to 30 cigarettes per day (300 across the entire baseline phase) and their 25% reduction measure became 21 cigarettes per day. When Participant 3 advanced to the 25% reduction + behavior plan phase, his range dropped to 12-

22 cigarettes per day for a total of 226 cigarettes for that phase and an average of 16 cigarettes per day. This 24.6% reduction was within the 5% threshold to advance to the 50% reduction phase. While in the 50% reduction function based phase, Participant 3's rate of continued to decrease. His range dropped to 8-15 cigarettes per day for a total of 171 cigarettes for that phase and an average of 12 cigarettes per day. This 43% reduction was outside of the 5% threshold to advance to the 75% reduction phase and Participant 3 moved back to Baseline.

While in the Return to

Baseline, Participant 3's behavior began to accelerate, ranging between 10-21 cigarettes per day for a total of 203 cigarettes for the phase and an average of 14.5 cigarettes per day. When advancing to the voucher based phase, Participant 3's behavior immediately came under the control of the new condition(s) and the trend reversed from the previous baseline. In the voucher based phase, his range dropped to 8-17 cigarettes per day for a total of 309 cigarettes and an average of 11 cigarettes per day for the 4 week phase. Overall the voucher based condition resulted in a 48.5% reduction from baseline. The CO tests for Participant 3 correlated very closely with the number of reported cigarettes across all phases, in addition, all cotinine tests were failed through the entire study (12 weeks) and suggests accuracy in reporting. While Participant 3 was unsuccessful in attaining 100% cessation, the selection of his own intervention in the voucher based phase(s) resulted in a 43% reduction, which equates to eliminating 65.5 cigarettes a week, or 13 packs of cigarettes a month. From a harm reduction standpoint this amount of reduction is extremely significant and it demonstrates the potential effectiveness of the participant's treatment plan which was developed off the functional assessment. Had the experiment continued this participant may have continued to reduce his rate of even further.

The voucher based phase did also decrease behavior to 48.5% relative to baseline. Given that this is a heavily researched methodology (voucher based progressive/resetting contingencies for cessation) and was successful in decreasing further. However, this treatment was not as successful at rapid deceleration in that the 50% reduction function based phase, and this participant was only slightly under the success criterion (7%) to advance to the 75% reduction phase.

One consideration for this participant is regarding the core methodology of this particular study, cessation in the absence of nicotine replacement. The behavior plan that was developed in collaboration with this participant directly addressed the functions that were reflected in assessment results, except for one: Automatic Negative (Remove Withdrawal & Avoid Withdrawal). Given study Institutional Review Board constraints, a standardized titration plan was used instead of any form of nicotine replacement and the assumption was that a titration plan would be effective for participants that had this result. However, when analyzing assessment results there were 120 "strongly agree/agree" statements across the sub-categories, and Reduce Withdrawal & Avoid Withdrawal were both values of 7. These responses strongly indicate a nicotine access function (escape/avoid withdrawal). As far as multiple control goes, there is a very real possibility that a potentially ineffective treatment like titration may not reduce cigarette consumption for this particular function, relative to the other escape functions reflected in assessment. In the event this study was able to utilize some form of nicotine replacement, a titration plan may have been more successful, since Participant 3 would no longer be experiencing high levels of nicotine withdrawal.

An important to note regarding Participant 3 is that he never received an increase in voucher amount and only 10 CO vouchers were ever delivered. All of these vouchers were at $.25 level, meaning 74 tests were failed and/or not submitted. In effect, every semi-weekly follow-up in this phase (8) involved the presentation of aversive control through the resetting contingency. However,, this participant submitted every single cotinine test (8) as well. In research of this nature, the response effort to submit self-management data takes time and energy. Participant 3 continued the study despite regularly missing access to vouchers. Despite the punitive consequences, Participant 3's reporting behavior was not suppressed. Overall, both the function based and voucher based intervention(s) were successful in reducing overall rates, however it is also unclear if Participant 3 continued to utilize the behavior plan, if their behavior came under control of the progressive-resetting contingency, or it was a product of both. Again, from a harm reduction standpoint, even though this participant was not successful in full cessation, Participant 3's rate of did significantly decrease, and this certainly is a meaningful behavior change that may decrease the probability of long term negative health effects.

Participant 4

Participant 4's assessment results indicated primarily Attention and Automatic Negative functions with Other's Request from the Attention function and Reduce Stress and Remove Thoughts from the Automatic Negative function. The behavior plan established for Participant 4 was as follows: "Increase activities like spending quality time with others, working on creative projects (design, styling, hair, makeup, nails), maintaining a regular routine (with agendas), and going to the gym." In discussing this behavior plan with the participant, there was not a need to specifically target the Attention function since components of this treatment relating to competing/incompatible responses would already be occurring. By creating a reinforcer rich environment as an alternative to (for Reduce Stress & Remove Thoughts), the access to a primary reinforcer (drug) may be competed with by a multitude of secondary reinforcer(s) that would. Lastly, the Participant's intervention included a standardized planned titration component as this research focus is cessation in the absence of nicotine replacement. Participant 4's selfreport (Table 9) identified "death related & trauma" as the primary maintaining variable and did not specifically identify an

Attention function nor other components of an automatic negative function.

Participant 4's baseline was the standard length (2 weeks) Participant 4 engaged in low levels of ranging from 0 to 5 cigarettes per day (20 across the entire baseline phase). and their goal in the 25% reduction function based phase was 0.7 cigarettes per day (10/week). In baseline, Participant 4's data were on a steady downtrend. After 5 days of intervention, the Participant 4 no longer submitted any CO tests, cotinine tests, or the number of cigarettes consumed per day. This participant's CO tests and cotinine tests appear to be consistent with the self-report data on the number of cigarettes consumed, suggesting accuracy in reporting. Projecting the data for the function based 25% reduction phase suggest that Participant 4 would have met the 25% reduction criterion and advanced to the 50% reduction phase had they continued in the study. It is not possible to ascertain if the 25% reduction + behavior plan phase had any effect given that behavior began to decrease in bassline while tracking and selfreporting data (number of Cigarettes, CO, and Cotinine). levels reached (0-1) by the second week of baseline which is also where the number of cigarettes remained by the

first

Friday of intervention. The results are inconclusive if the participant's

treatment plan, which was developed off the functional assessment

was an effective measure for function.

Research Question Discussion

The objective of this research was to compare the effects of

function-based treatment packages developed with the input of

participants on self-reported frequency of , levels of CO, and levels of

salivary cotinine to those of voucher-based reinforcement.

Additionally, adherence to each treatment package (i.e., an

assessment of procedural fidelity and accuracy of self-reported

function). In other words, did the assessment correctly identify the

function, and result in decreases of with high fidelity in following the

function based treatment which would indicate that the function

assessed by the plan was correct.

Based on the assumed function-based treatment packages, the

validity of an indirect functional assessment in identifying the

function of behavior was discussed.

For Participant 1, the function-based treatment was successful in completely suppressing behavior and this cessation continued through one-month follow-up. For Participant 2, the function-based treatment was effective from a harm reduction standpoint by significantly decreasing his frequency of in the environment (bar) that evoked this behavior and the individuals that occasioned it (given primarily socially mediated). At one-month follow-up, Participant 3 reported that he continued to smoke but his total frequency was significantly decreased. For Participant 3, the function-based treatment was effective from a harm reduction standpoint by significantly decreasing his across all environments, at one-month follow-up, the Participant 3 reported that they continued to smoke, but their rate of was more or less where it was when we finished the study (Table 8). For Participant 4, the results of the function-based treatment are inconclusive as Participant 4 did not continue submitting data after the first Friday of the treatment phase. However, data they did submit was within the goal range. Participants 2 and 3 both advanced to the Voucher-based phase, and both were successful at decreasing their further relative to the 50% reduction + behavior plan phase. In all, both treatments appear to be effective at decreasing

. However, based on all participant data, only Participant 1 was able to achieve full cessation, and that was with the function-based treatment. Depending on the reasons/functions for an individual's behavior, voucher or function based may not be effective for automatic functions related to withdrawal, and those individuals may need to use nicotine replacement.

General Discussion

Every participant reduced during the function based 25% reduction phase compared to baseline, which may indicate that the functional assessment successfully identified variables related to all participant's behavior and meaningfully informed an effective behavior analytic treatment. At a minimum, these respective behavior plans and progressive titration reduced the number of cigarettes consumed for all participants and promoted full suppression in the case of Participant 1. Additionally, Participant 1's recovery of (1 cigarette in the final phase) is exemplified by Silverman and colleagues (2008) who discussed the notion that individuals' abstinence may lapse (intermittently consume a tobacco product) and still be successful in a cessation effort. This adds strength to non-punishment based interventions where behavior can still be intermittently reinforced and treatment may still be successful.

Despite the significant daily response requirement as related to data collection in this study, participants were incredibly reliable in submitting their tests for the minimal compensation that was provided. Additionally, the modest reinforcement promoted accurate reporting as evidenced by the individual video phase check-ins and cotinine test results. There were no negative consequences associated with failed tests during the function based phases as the submission of a test resulted in voucher delivery regardless of result. For Participant 2 and 3, the punitive consequence in the voucher based phase of resetting vouchers and non-delivery of vouchers for failed tests did not suppress reporting, which adds strength to the learning history developed for regular submission of tests throughout this study.

Several participants self-reported that the immediate feedback given from the carbon monoxide device was enjoyable, independent of voucher delivery. Participant 1 said, "why is my value not zero", when he had reached the level of full cessation and also a comment of "this monitoring process makes you cautious not to smoke lol". The researcher shared with Participant 1 that carbon monoxide is in the air, which is why values of ≤4ppm were considered to be level of a non-smoker.

In assessing the repeatability of measures in the functional assessment, there were zero instances where participants scored the same positive and negative values in a respective subfunction. Each sub-function included six variants to the same question, and if participants scored each of these values the same, these questions may be seen as equivalent. This notion was important in testing the effectiveness in a question's ability to correspond to a particular subfunction. Given this result, this adds strength to the effective counterbalancing of question wording. If questions were perfectly counterbalanced, the assessment length could be significantly truncated to include 1-3 questions per sub-function instead of 6. Additionally, no participant scored Remove Pain (physical) as a maintaining variable.

The Escape functions were a testament to this concept in that the behavior of may occur as a means to escape/avoid a task, remove boredom, or as an activity while the individual is in transit. None of these functions necessarily involve a social mediator but they are certainly not an automatically maintained biological function related to avoiding or escaping withdrawal.

As for the measures utilized, salivary cotinine tests are sensitive to nicotine metabolites broken down in the liver and CO tests are sensitive to blood carbon monoxide levels through exhaling. Given that these two measures are both collateral to , they were highly effective measures to assess cessation progress, especially when collected in tandem and on regular intervals which were paired to the half-life of those biological biproducts.

While the participant pool was small, participants were culturally, geographically, and generationally diverse. One participant was Asian, two participants were White, and one participant was Black. Their ages were 38, 51, 45, and 36, respectively. Additionally, all participants had vastly different functional assessment results. Participant 1's behavior was predominantly maintained by Automatic Negative functions regarding stress and Escape from aversive stimulation. Participant 2's behavior was predominantly maintained by Attention access. Participant 3's behavior was predominantly maintained by Escape from aversive stimulation and Automatic Negative functions regarding stress and withdrawal symptoms.

Participant 4's behavior was maintained predominantly by the Automatic Negative function regarding stress. All of this considered, Participant 3 was the only individual whose results suggested a nicotine based function. With these individual assessment results in mind, the default treatment of nicotine replacement for any individual that wishes to reach the level of full cessation may not be the most effective treatment, as this may not be the primary maintaining variable for all individuals despite being an addictive drug. Conversely, for those who have this function, cessation may not be successful without nicotine replacement.

Existing literature suggests that Voucher based reinforcement is an incredibly powerful tool for promoting cessation. This study was most similar to Dallery and Glenn (2005) where an internet based cessation protocol was utilized with the vouchers being contingent upon abstinence, and similarly, all participants also saw a sustained decrease in CO levels/number of cigarettes relative to baseline. This study also included many components from Dallery et al. (2013) as it relates to the effectiveness of feedback, monitoring, and goal setting.

Voucher based reinforcement is a contingent presentation of a GCR which may overpower any reinforcing functions or multiple control regarding the itself by providing access to a valuable secondary reinforcer. Contingent electric shock is an unconditioned punisher and may not be the most ethical means to promote long-term cessation, as it has been shown to be maximally invasive and maximally restrictive (Lerman & Vorndran, 2002). With both of these treatments in mind, there is a significant value added if function based treatments can be effective in promoting cessation and data from this study contribute to the scientific literature in that regard.

Participants showed a reduction in throughout their baseline phases and this is consistent with existing literature regarding tracking of a target behavior in self-management plans. Additionally, across all participants, carryover effects may have been an unintended consequence. For Participant 3 in particular, his rate of continued to remain at the levels consistent with the previous condition following return to baseline. However,, this phase was on an overall uptrend as his behavior came under control of the second baseline condition by the second week. Both Participants 2 and 3 received the voucher based treatment, and as mentioned above, there is no way to ascertain if those participants continued to utilize the self-management methodologies from the behavior plan while in Voucher based treatment. In this phase participants were instructed to use any means they wish to completely eliminate . An important note is that no participant reported any nicotine replacement as an intervention in the Voucher Based phase.

Voucher based treatment in this study included the criterion of full cessation on a daily basis and was significantly too high for Participant 3 when considering his baseline data. Participant 3 may have been more successful in his cessation goals if the vouchers were contingent upon a progressive, percentage-based reduction rather than full cessation. Additionally, if the study had utilized a 10% reduction per week Participant 3 may have been more successful over time. Unfortunately, this type of treatment was not an option given the research questions of the current study relating to the effectiveness of standardized titration embedded within an individualized behavior plan. Additionally, if this Participant 3 had received a different intervention than his counterparts, this would have created a confound for the study. Participant 1 was the only individual to reach full cessation; however, their data collection fidelity was the lowest of all participants. With this in mind, data collection fidelity is not necessarily indicative of treatment success. Participant 3 consistently had the highest data collection fidelity. At the same time, Participant 3 also consumed significantly more cigarettes throughout the duration of the study than any other participant. However, Participant 3 also had the greatest reduction in number of cigarettes consumed, across all participants.

From what the research suggests regarding intermittently reinforced behavior being incredibly resilient (citation), Participant 2's , especially within the context of collateral reinforcement (alcohol) is an incredibly difficult behavior to intervene upon as the behavior does not occur every single day, and when it does, it occurs at incredibly high rates. Additionally, alcohol may play a role in the potential degradation of self-management effectiveness.

In all, function based treatment for cessation has promise, but a concern for this treatment is that titration plans (if utilized) should not be standardized, they should be individualized to the participant's own baseline data. In the case of Participant 2 and 3, both participants may have been more successful in reducing their cigarette consumption if their goals involved smaller decreases which would ultimately lead to more success/reinforcement to build momentum as opposed to a time based titration plan.

Study Limitations

Recruitment Limitations

This study included a total of four participants. Three participants completed the entire study but only two experienced the function based vs voucher based treatment. Given the low N, more research would be required to fully assess the effectiveness of the function based treatment.

Pre-Assessment Limitations

The pre-assessment should have included additional questions and some questions should be modified. Marijuana "products" was an exclusionary criterion and one individual was not able to participate in the study due to their use of "edibles." Although this is not a marijuana product that is smoked this participant was still excluded. Additionally, the pre-assessment should have asked questions such as "what brand of cigarette do you smoke, how much of a cigarette do you regularly consume (e.g., single drag, 25%, 50%, etc.)", both as an assessment of nicotine levels. Additionally, the assessment should have asked if the participant(s) were going to have any extended travel (domestic or international). Information on travel may have resulted in a study start delay as baseline data may during travel may not necessarily mirror baseline data in one's regular environment. In the case of Participant 1 & 2, the behavior of was suppressed during travel, which occurred in the first baselines. At the same time, for Participant 2, the data suggested no during the week and very high rates on the weekend, which was still reflected, despite the travel.

Functional Assessment Limitations

When the assessment was created, the primary researcher understood the collateral nature of alcohol and cigarettes. For Participant 2, the result was a spike in "attention" function and while developing the behavior plan these evocative stimuli were easily identified but not specifically identified by the functional assessment. At final debriefing, Participant 2 also expressed a desire for questions related to alcohol be asked within the assessment. With this in mind, an assessment of this nature (while comprehensive) may benefit by adding a 4th category of evocative stimuli. Given that this is a novel assessment, it is unknown if each question was worded in a way that would weight each response equally (e.g., repeatability and reliability of the question), although 6 questions were added for this precise reason, to mitigate these potential effects.

Technological & Response Measurement Limitations

The intended CO tests for this study were iPhone/Android connected and relatively inexpensive ($60) in addition to being good for 200 uses. In the time of this study's creation, and during COVID, these devices were no longer available within the United States. At this time, new medical grade CO tests were procured ($620) in addition to additional breath tubes (single use) and a canister of CO for re-calibration. Given the cost of carbon monoxide reader devices only a limited number were purchased for this study (5). Within several weeks, Participant 1's device degraded to the level that it was no longer functional. This resulted in a (3) day period where data were unable to be collected. There was no set plan established for participant outreach in the event a device became non-functional. Additionally, cotinine tests were of a significant expense ($255/case of 30) and global supply chains related to COVID required the primary researcher to pivot to a different device. The original cotinine test assessed levels of cotinine in the participant's blood (saliva test) and this measure would have been significantly more meaningful than the pass/fail cotinine test selected for this study. It is important to note that these cotinine tests had not reached the date of expiry prior to individual study conclusion(s). Participant 2, started data collection several days before Participant 1, received a cotinine test box that had the earliest expiration (one-month prior to his study conclusion). Additionally,

Participant 1 reported that toward the end of the study several of his tests returned "invalid" results and he was able to complete an additional test which did produce a pass/fail response. There were also two instances of Participant 1 reporting their cotinine test failed to produce a result and that they needed to complete another. Additionally, the researcher did not specify what a participant should do in the event a cotinine test had returned an invalid result.

While the study collected Cotinine tests twice per week the submission of these tests were not always on the same exact day(s), although, consistently separated by several days to add more strength to the data collected, participant(s) should have been required to submit (3) cotinine tests a week instead of (2).

As for response measurement, this study did not collect data on the percentage of a cigarette that was consumed, one drag or more was considered a full cigarette as far as the activity of was considered. Other studies have collected this data and their inclusion may have been meaningful addition (COVID aside).

Nicotine Replacement Limitations

Given constraints imposed by the Institutional Review Board (IRB), the primary researcher was unable to utilize any form of nicotine replacement (e.g., patches, gum, etc.) When assessing each individual's assumed function a general titration plan was imposed for each participant as an alternative. Although, no participant reported utilizing nicotine replacement methods in their voucher based phase (participants independently selected any intervention of their choice). Given Participant 3's data, there is a strong case to be made that his intervention would have been significantly augmented by nicotine replacement as that was one of the primary functions he reported. At the same time, the interventions assessing all other function(s) did result in a significant reduction. In all, not providing the ability for participants to use additional nicotine replacement methods may have limited participants' success in reducing behavior.

Experimental Design Limitations

The study was created with the intention that every participant would follow the same treatment progression (e.g., baseline, function based, return to baseline, if needed, and then an advancement to voucher based treatment). While every participant did follow this progression, Participant 1 had an extended baseline (one month). Participant 2 and 3 had made progress toward their 50% reduction goal, but ultimately failed to meet advancement criterion to the 75% reduction phase. Given more time, or utilizing smaller, but still progressive titration goals, the participant(s) data suggest that the behavior of would have continued on the respective downtrend and they would have been successful during the 75% reduction phase. However, dynamically adjusting criterion based on participant data would have added a major limitation to this study as titration plans would have been different for all participants and limiting conclusions about the effectiveness of function based treatment phase. Additionally, this would mean that different functions (across participants) would have had different length of treatment further limiting conclusions about function based treatment effectiveness.

Future Research

As mentioned above, future research should assess the total amount of a cigarette consumed to more accurately assess nicotine levels and during the pre-assessment phase for participant(s). This would allow participants to self-report the number and percentage of cigarettes they consume each day to compare against true baseline data. Additionally, researchers should review if dynamically adjusting criterion for cessation would be more effective than static phases and ensure that the behavior of fully comes under control of the current condition prior to advancement to a progressively lower criterion or a failure to meet criterion. For response measurement, researchers should continue to use the medical grade CO tests and if possible procure the cotinine tests that directly assess the cotinine levels in the participant's bloodstream (saliva). For the future of the functional assessment, researchers should identify if questions are equally weighted and if they are to reduce the assessment length. Additionally, this assessment required the primary researcher to assess the data and develop a behavior plan with the individual. It may be possible to automate the process by adding an additional category to the assessment regarding evocative/occasioning stimuli to eliminate the need for a researcher developed behavior plan. As for social significance, future researchers should assess the effects of a behavior plan that is auto-generated (as described above), vs the methodology utilized in this study where the participant was an active participant in their own research. Future researchers should be aware of the potential effects of participant dropout related to providing video evidence or producing 300+ tests for staying in the study. Additionally, future researchers should look at shortening the length of the study. Given that there were there were no programmed negative consequences associated with submitting a failed test in the function based phase, participants were being incentivized to report accurately and this was verified by the cotinine tests. Future researchers should

continue to use these two measurements in tandem.